AF148772

POLITICS TRUMPS ECONOMICS

POLITICS TRUMPS ECONOMICS

The Interface of Economics and
Politics in Contemporary India

Edited by
BIMAL JALAN
PULAPRE BALAKRISHNAN

RAINLIGHT
RUPA

Published in Rainlight
by Rupa Publications India Pvt. Ltd 2014
7/16, Ansari Road, Daryaganj
New Delhi 110002

Sales centres:
Allahabad Bengaluru Chennai
Hyderabad Jaipur Kathmandu
Kolkata Mumbai

Edition Copyright © Bimal Jalan and Pulapre Balakrishnan 2014

Copyright for individual pieces vests with the respective authors.

All rights reserved.
No part of this publication may be reproduced, transmitted, or stored in
a retrieval system, in any form or by any means, electronic, mechanical,
photocopying, recording or otherwise, without the prior permission
of the publisher.

ISBN: 978-81-291-3273-4

First impression 2014
10 9 8 7 6 5 4 3 2 1

The moral right of the author has been asserted.

Typeset in 10/13 Sabon by RECTO Graphics, Delhi.

This book is sold subject to the condition that it shall not,
by way of trade or otherwise, be lent, resold, hired out, or otherwise circulated,
without the publisher's prior consent, in any form of binding or cover
other than that in which it is published.

Contents

Preface

Till only a couple of years ago, India's reputation, both as the world's largest democracy and a rising economic power, was at its peak. Today, with daily reports of a declining growth rate, widespread corruption, failure in the delivery of essential services and public despair over the content of politics, the picture has changed dramatically. The perception of India seems to have swung from one of a land of great opportunity to that of a country with an uncertain future.

That India's full potential is not being actualized to make way for a dynamic economy and acceptable living conditions for its people points to something other than mere economics being at play. And this is the ever-present politics. This conclusion may be arrived at via a process of elimination, for nothing else can be the answer to the rhetorical question, why in this country a globally impressive talent pool coexists with the highest incidence of poverty in the world. We believe that the engaged Indian is concerned about this situation, wanting to know how it has come to be and what can be done to alleviate it.

This book attempts to provide an answer to the question posed above. While the essays contained in it are on diverse topics, all of them engage with the interface between politics and economics in their chosen subject area, demonstrating how politics often impinges upon economics whether in the making of public policy or in its implementation. While recognition of the role of political economy has long made it *de riguer* for social analysts to acknowledge the influence of political considerations in policy making, it is not sufficiently well recognized that politics can also influence the outcome of policies however well-intentioned. This it does via the nature of governance.

We have reason to believe this, as even in the recent past higher growth rates have been secured from levels of domestic investment lower than what it is currently. In other words, the productivity of investment could have declined. Governance can impinge upon productivity as much of the infrastructure in India is in the public sector. Private economic activity, not to mention private investment, is closely tied to the availability of the producer services that flow from infrastructure. The role of governance in the provision of these infrastructural services is well captured by the maxim: 'It is not how much you have but how you use it'.

Effective governance is particularly essential at a time when India is becoming more integrated with the rest of the world—inheriting the opportunities along with the threats—and faces a major challenge in the form of a natural resource base under pressure. Now it must be that governance is also understood as adapting public policy to what an economy needs at any point in time. It is therefore essential to both widen the conventional understanding of 'governance', and to recognize the role of politics in determining the outcome of policies, both economic and social. This accounts for the origin of the idea for this book. It brings together a set of thinkers who are at the forefront of their own chosen subject areas. As leaders in their respective professions they may be expected to have thrown authoritative light on the topics on which they have written here.

It gives us great pleasure to express our appreciation in equal measure to both our co-authors and the publisher. The former responded swiftly to our request for a paper subject to an unusually stringent timeline. To the publisher Rupa, represented by Ms Ritu Vajpeyi-Mohan, we are grateful for having conceived of this volume of essays and suggesting to us a suitable title. Ms Dharini Bhaskar was a most helpful and efficient copyeditor to us. Mr T. J. Emmanuel liased on our behalf with the authors and the publisher and Ms Deepmala assisted with preparation of the manuscript. Finally, for support received, Balakrishnan expresses his appreciation to the Centre for Development Studies at Thiruvananthapuram and to the Indian Statistical Institute at Delhi where this project was initiated and completed, respectively.

Bimal Jalan
Pulapre Balakrishnan

New Delhi
4 February 2014

POLITICS

Chapter 1

Overview

Bimal Jalan

Since 2011, India has been the world's third largest economy in 'purchasing power parity' terms. Size bestows several advantages on an economy such as a higher scale of production, with all its attendant benefits, including access to a high stock of human capital and higher productivity. That these potential advantages are not materializing in India today—and that India continues to have the largest number of persons below the poverty line in the world—points to something other than mere economics which is slowing the pace of growth and poverty alleviation in India. And this factor is ever-present politics.

India's history since independence, as indeed that of other developing countries across the world, highlights the importance of politics to outcomes. In this context, an additional factor which needs to be kept in view is that the overall political situation changes from time to time, for better or for worse, which in turn affects the economy. As observed by the famous economist Gunnar Myrdal in the early years of development planning, 'the only certainty is that we shall be continuously surprised by seeing the unexpected

happen. Nothing is permanent, particularly political development'
(Myrdal 1957).

In considering the factors which have adversely affected India's
economic growth in recent years, an important development that
needs to be taken into account is the changed nature of politics.
The emergence of multi-party coalitions at the Centre has meant
a disproportionate influence of small regional parties without an
articulated agenda, lack of 'collective' responsibility and reduced
accountability of the government in the delivery of public services.

The main objective of the essays in this book is to highlight the
importance of adapting economic policies to the evolving situation
in terms of what the economy needs at any point of time rather
than adopting differential policies dictated by different ministries,
depending on the wishes and special interests of individual ministers
representing multiple small parties in a coalition government.
In a democracy, any programme for change must also be fully
supported by the people in general and not only by the politicians
in power. In this Overview, I propose to highlight a few core issues
relating to the emerging crisis of governance in the administrative
and political system, and what needs to be done to improve the
working of the government in India for the benefit of the economy.

A fundamental 'systemic' change, which dominates the
working of India's politics today—unlike in the first four decades
after independence—is the emergence of coalitions as the 'normal'
form of government since 1989. India has had as many as nine
governments during the past 23 years with an average life of less
than two and a half years. Of these, three multi-party coalitions
survived their five-year terms with occasional setbacks and shifts in
the composition of parties supporting them from inside or outside.
Excluding these three and the government in office at the time
of writing, the United Progressive Alliance (UPA) coalition, the
average term of five governments—with enormous powers to
allocate resources, control public enterprises and decide inter-state
allocation of investments—was less than one year.

It does not take a political genius to recognize that if he or she
is in politics and gets elected to Parliament or a state legislature, his

or her life expectancy in office is likely to be 'short' and entirely dependent on the party leader, unless, of course, he or she happens to be that leader or a direct descendent of the leader.

The crucial point here is that at the time of forming a multi-party coalition government, the expectations of small and regional parties are that the enormous powers that their nominees, as ministers, enjoy may not last very long or that this may change if a more powerful leader of one of the larger parties in the coalition so decides.

Under the present constitutional provisions, as a consequence of amendments made in 1985 to prevent defections, and again in 2003, there is now also a built-in incentive for fragmentation of political parties at the time of elections. This is because the smaller a party, the greater the power of an individual legislator to defect to another party in search of political power without having to relinquish his or her seat in Parliament or in a state assembly. On the other hand, a member elected from a large national party has very little discretion to defect without the support of a substantial number of other members, who also wish to defect. Thus, the smaller a party, the easier it is for a few of its members or all of them to switch from one coalition to another, and maximize their 'political reward'. The same is true of so-called 'independent' members, who are supported by some political party during elections. So, in a situation where multi-party coalitions are the norm, all regional or caste leaders naturally have a greater incentive to form their own separate parties.

In addition to fragmentation of parties and a short life expectancy of coalition governments at birth, there has also been a subtle change in the role of Parliament and the accountability of the executive to Parliament in recent years. The Parliament now has multiple 'power centres' (in addition to the party leading the government, and the party leading the opposition). An important consequence of the emergence of multiple centres of power is that what Parliament does or does not do depends on 'behind the scene' agreements among different sets of party leaders within and outside the government. As long as the government has the backing of a sufficient number of leaders, it is supreme and it can get Parliament to do what it wishes. The implication of this is that, as noted historian and political analyst Eric Hobsbawm, has pointed out in another context, when important national decisions are taken among small groups of people in private in a democracy, the position is not very different from the way they would have been taken in the absence of democracy.

Unfortunately, over the past two decades in particular, politics has also become a career of choice for persons with criminal records. The investigative and prosecution machinery for suspected criminal activities is under the direct control of departments in the government. There is a natural reluctance to speed up investigations and the prosecution of persons who are leaders of political parties and/or members of the cabinet. According to the statistical survey of the recent elections to the Lok Sabha, it was found that nearly 20 per cent of the candidates surveyed, cutting across party lines, (excluding independent candidates) had criminal antecedents. In the Lok Sabha, which has 543 seats in all, over the past several years, well over 100 members have had criminal cases pending against them. No wonder that physical scuffles and assaults among some members on the floor of state assemblies, and even Parliament, is not an uncommon sight when tempers rise because of charges of corruption and wrong-doing by leaders of one political party or another.

Further, unlike other democracies, in addition to major industries like oil, gas and steel, public sector enterprises in India are dominant in the financial field (particularly banking and insurance) and transport (particularly railways, ports and airports). The awarding of contracts as well as operational priorities, in addition to appointments, are subject to ministerial discretion without sufficient accountability. Naturally, discretionary allocation of public resources has tremendous significance for the functioning of the economy.

Recently, there has been widespread public outrage over corrupt ministers at the Centre and in the states about scams relating to the allocation of natural resources such as land, mines and gas. Some ministers have also been sent to jail by the Supreme Court because of their involvement in bribery and other unacceptable practices. To see our so-called Hon'ble ministers in jail is a sad commentary on the functioning of India's democracy. But let us also ask ourselves—how is it that these elected representatives of the people had the opportunity and such enormous discretionary powers to accept massive bribes from corrupt corporates? Who gave them this opportunity? Was it the intention of the framers of our Constitution to confer such powers on elected representatives of the people?

A fundamental principle laid down in our Constitution in Article 75(3) is that 'The Council of Ministers shall be collectively responsible to the House of the People.' However, recent history is full of instances where important policy decisions, leading to considerable revenue loss to the government and/or unwarranted allocation of public resources for personal gain by political leaders, have been taken without 'collective responsibility'. A striking example is with respect to the allocation of 2G Spectrum—heads of ministries, which were involved in the process of allocation have been 'passing the buck', as it were, to some other ministry or to their own civil servants on the ground that they merely concurred in the decision taken by someone else. It has also been claimed that in any case, the final decision was approved by the cabinet. If this was indeed the case, then the question arises: what exactly does the 'collective responsibility' of the cabinet mean?

It is abundantly clear that unless Indian authorities are forced to take measures to improve governance and halt the 'demand and supply' of corruption in the economy, there is simply no way in which India can reduce the rising disparity (and despair) among its people. Given the current political scenario of multiple-party coalitions with no shared agenda, dramatic reforms or 'hard' measures to improve administrative efficiency may not be feasible in the near future. However, hopefully, with emerging pressure from civil society, it should be possible to evolve a consensus on introducing a package of reforms which are relatively benign and are likely to be in the overall interest of the country as a whole over the next few years.

A major step in this direction has been the enactment of the Right to Information Act, 2005. The beneficial impact of this legislation in making the government accountable and citizen-friendly is already visible. A further desirable step is making it mandatory for all ministries and departments of the government to voluntarily make information (excluding security-related subjects) on the decisions taken by them available to the public. It may be clarified that information should be released by the ministries themselves without the need for any member of the public to ask for it. If this is done, free media and civil society institutions will constitute an effective instrument for enforcing accountability in the decision-making process itself.

In addition to administrative reforms and improving the performance of governments when in power, it is also necessary to introduce some political reforms to reduce corruption, the power of small parties to destabilize multi-party coalitions and attractiveness of politics as a career for persons with criminal antecedents. I have dealt with these and other political issues which require urgent attention in some detail elsewhere (see *India's Politics: A View from the Backbench*, Penguin, 2007). So let me only mention a couple of urgent political reforms which require to be undertaken as early as possible.

First, the anti-defection law should also be made applicable to small parties and independent members who choose to join the government. Essentially, those who join the government ought not to be allowed to defect (as has happened in several states in the past few years) without having to seek re-election. At present, as mentioned earlier, there is a built-in incentive for fragmentation of political parties at the time of elections in order to avoid the need to seek re-election in case a party decides to defect from the ruling coalition. Thus, if a member belonging to a large national party does not follow the directions or whip issued by his party, he/she may be expelled from the party and will have to seek re-election. However, if the same person is a member of a small party of five or 10 members, a consensus among them to defect and switch from one coalition to another without losing their seats is permitted. This has had the unintended consequence of providing an incentive for forming small parties and reducing the personal autonomy of elected legislators belonging to a large party.

Secondly, highest priority should be given by courts to hear cases of elected leaders with criminal antecedents. Their cases should be mandatorily adjudicated within six months of their election. Such a procedure will effectively 'reverse' the incentive for criminals to choose politics in order to delay investigations in their cases and also possible conviction. In fact, they may choose not to contest elections so that they are in a position to delay hearings through normal legal procedures!

There is, of course, a lot more that needs to be done to improve the working of our politics to realize India's full economic potential as one of the fastest growing market economies in the world. This is the primary objective of putting together a set of essays in this volume on various aspects of the interface between politics and economics in contemporary India. At present, fractious politics trumps economics in the country. Even with all its advantages in terms of skills, technology, manpower and entrepreneurial excellence, India's rank in the Human Development Index (HDI) remains among the bottom one-third of the countries in the world. Thus, in the latest HDI Index, released by United Nations in 2013, India's rank was as low as 136 out of 186 countries. As we look ahead, the primary challenge before us is how to make India perform better, and thereby substantially raise its HDI ranking among countries across the world.

The 12 essays in this book, including this Overview, are categorized into three sections: Politics, Governance and Policy. All the three aspects are, of course, closely inter-related as politics determines governance and policymaking. Governance in turn determines outcomes and successful policymaking has a substantial impact on the shape of politics in all economies.

Essays on different aspects of politics, governance and policy in this volume have been contributed by eminent economists, political analysts and policymakers with academic and/or professional experience. I should mention that all the authors, who graciously agreed to contribute to this volume, have given their personal views in their essays. No attempt was made by the editors of the volume, or for that matter the publisher, to coordinate or develop a consensus on the views expressed by them on different subjects. However, as it happens, there is some commonality of views among different authors on several crucial and over-arching aspects of India's current problems and what needs to be done to resolve them.

So far as the country's economic prospects are concerned, a common thread running through most of the essays is that contrary to popular belief which dominates the media, the main problem is not the so-called 'policy paralysis' or lack of macroeconomic policy reforms. It is simply that, over time, India's administrative system has become largely 'non-functional' and non-responsive to the interests of an average citizen. So far as policymaking is concerned, there is actually a plethora of announcements and documents, including voluminous Five Year Plans, on every conceivable economic issue. What India actually lacks is not the supply of policies but their lackadaisical implementation, which is next to impossible, or at best difficult to track over time. It is the administrative bottlenecks and plethora of agencies and public institutions involved in the implementation of announced policies which explain most of the problems that India's economy faces—ranging from non-delivery of public services to widespread corruption at different levels and lack of sufficient public resources required for investments at the Centre as well as in the states. Let us take, for example, public delivery of services and corruption. According to estimates made by the Planning Commission, nearly 48 per cent of the foodgrains released through the public distribution system at subsidized prices are actually diverted and do not reach the poor. All the collection agencies involved in the task of distributing food to the poor—from the Centre to the states to the districts—are government agencies, and yet they fail to reduce the levels of corruption and diversion. As is well-recorded, central and state governments have more than 100 separate schemes with large budgetary allocations for delivering education, water, health, sewage, sanitation and shelter, in addition to food, to the poor and yet India continues to have the largest number of deprived persons on any measure of poverty or human development.

So far as the level and spread of corruption is concerned, several essays in this volume highlight the rising supply and demand of corruption in almost all segments of the economy, not only among political classes, but in the country as a whole irrespective of the educational or professional background of the people. It also affects tax collection and implementation of announced fiscal policies for achieving the intended social priorities. As a result, a considerable portion of public-sector spending has to be financed from borrowing, leading to large deficits and debt. Unfortunately, even rising levels of public spending have failed to create the physical and social infrastructure required to propel investments to accelerate growth and reduce poverty to the desired extent. The recent experience of fiscal adjustment also brings to the fore the need for a robust institutional arrangement for monitoring the fiscal behaviour of the government. However, while institutional arrangements will strengthen fiscal behaviour, ultimately it is political will that is necessary for a stable and sustainable public finance policy in India.

While these problems cause considerable difficulties for an average citizen, several essays also suggest measures which can be taken by the government to improve the situation. A primary reason for poor delivery of public services at the ground level is believed to be due to over-centralization of administrative and governance powers in the hands of the central government vis-à-vis the state governments, which have the primary responsibility of delivering the services to the people. In order to improve the working of the present system, it has been suggested that it is essential to make 'systemic' changes in terms of transfer of administrative powers to the states in several critical areas, particularly agriculture, education, health and internal security.

Reducing the scale and motives for corruption also call for a multi-pronged approach combining reforms at different levels, strategies to elicit the support of all the relevant stakeholders and persistent public campaigns against corruption. It has also been suggested that among other measures, public funding of elections will be an effective way of minimizing the influence of money and corruption on the political system. Interestingly, the additional cost of public financing of elections over and above what is being distributed now by way of the Members of Parliament Local Area Development Scheme (MPLADS) funds among Members of Parliament (MPs) is unlikely to be significant.

While there is widespread acceptance of the idea of human rights as a guiding principle for judging the performance of political societies, another important suggestion is that the idea of equity should not be defined narrowly in terms of income and wealth inequality. While the concept of equity based on income is certainly relevant, it is even more important to pay attention to social equity, which is defined as the equality of rank or dignity of different groups in society. In India, since the beginning of development planning, the missing dimension has been a social profile of gainers and losers. Social equity is an important but often ignored dimension of inclusive development. It deserves to be incorporated in the government's planning for development of the country in the future.

Another important observation is that a large part of India's economy is in the informal and unorganized sectors, and as a result economic outcomes in terms of budgetary expenditure and subsidies depend on how the administrative system actually functions in small towns or villages. Unfortunately, at the bottom levels of the administrative pyramid, different parts of the government end up making different, and sometimes contradictory, interventions leading to policy incoherence and diversion of public resources.

There are several other suggestions, spread over different essays in the book, for improving the working of our political and economic system for the benefit of the people as a whole. But let me stop here and conclude this Overview on a somewhat more positive note.

Notwithstanding our past performance, I am sanguine about India's economic potential and our ability to achieve high growth with financial stability. The reason for this confidence is that despite problems in governance, the innate ability of our people is immense and has been demonstrated beyond reasonable doubt. The open, participatory and democratic system ensures that change can be delayed but it cannot be avoided altogether. If we act now, and if we are able to realize our full potential in the next 20 years, India's poverty will become a distant memory.

Reference

Myrdal, Gunnar. (1957). *Economic Theory and Underdeveloped Regions.* London: Methuen & Co.

Two Concepts of Equity

Meghnad Desai

Introduction

One of the most significant developments in political economy since the collapse of the Soviet Union is the increasing emphasis on the notions of rights and equity. The Cold War diverted much attention to the issues of communism versus capitalism, of state versus market and of freedom versus authoritarianism. Both sides were being hypocritical in the debate and hence there has been neither resolution nor progress in social thought.[1]

The elimination of the Leninist model as a serious alternative for the future has refocused attention on the only mode of production/social formation which the world has been left with—capitalism/liberal democracy, using both the words in their widest

---

[1] I have dealt with the history of the Cold War and the debates within Marxism in *Marx's Revenge: The Resurgence of Capitalism and the Death of Statist Socialism* (2002).

connotation. Issues of human rights and equity have re-emerged in public discourse.[2]

There is widespread acceptance of the idea of human rights as a guiding principle for judging the performance of political societies. However, the idea of equity has been translated somewhat narrowly into the idea of income/wealth inequality which is measured by a Gini coefficient. An earlier formulation by John Rawls put emphasis on the level of living of the 'worst off' in any society (Rawls 1971). This would take us to a poverty measure as a criterion of a good society. In this essay, I wish to argue that this is rather a narrow notion of equity. Prior to the idea of income or outcome equality, there has to be social equity defined as the equality of rank or dignity—social equality.

Social equality, or what I would prefer to label the equality of dignity, is a concept which has been subsumed as understood rather than defined. Modernity in Europe is assumed to have arrived after the demise of feudalism and the abolition of serfdom and other social ranks. While this is always a simplification, Karl Marx caught the essence of this in his Chapter 'Buying and Selling of Labour Power' (*Capital* Volume 1, Chapter 6). He took the view that the proletariat was free in a dual sense. He had been divorced—'freed'—from his access to the means of production, land in the first instance. But he was also free to move away from the demesne and enter into a contract to sell his labour power. Exchange relations are juridically equal although Marx was to highlight the class inequality of the participants in the exchange of labour power on either side. In his scheme of things the transition from feudalism to capitalism was preconditioned on the rise of free labour. Free labour had the equality of dignity in as much as the worker exchanged his labour power for money wages on conditions of equality.

---

[2] One indication of this is provided by the concept of human development and the universally favourable reception that the UNDP's Human Development reports have received.

Thus, the Marxian definition of capitalism as a mode of production presumes the existence of social equity. To the extent that such an equality of status does not prevail, the society in question bears marks of a pre-capitalist social formation. Even as advanced a capitalist nation as the US bore marks of its early dependence on slavery till the late twentieth century.

Social equality can thus co-exist with income inequality, class divisions and even some political disadvantage. The important point is that each member of a society can expect from everyone else an equality of respect, to be treated with dignity. This is easy to miss once it has been achieved because it becomes like breathing. But in many societies achieving social equality is the bigger and prior struggle than achieving economic equity. This is because even in mature modern societies, it is easy to find instances where the legal notions of social equality are not matched by daily behaviour. Much effort by non-governmental organizations (NGOs) and even the Commission on Equality in the UK, for instance, is about enforcing social equality norms be they across race, ethnicity, gender, lifestyles/fighting homophobia, disability, age and many other dimensions. The fight, however, is presumed upon the legal barriers having been broken down.

Not all societies satisfy the criterion of social equality. Just to take two simple examples. The US did not enjoy social equality between white and black Americans through much of the twentieth century; indeed not even when Rawls wrote his masterpiece on justice. It was achieved after a long struggle for civil rights during the decades of the 1950s, 1960s and 1970s. Issues of income inequality could not be addressed in the US without factoring in social inequality. While income inequality persists and the disadvantages of race have not been fully eliminated, there is no doubt that there is an equality of dignity across all races. The outrage felt when a black professor at Harvard was handled roughly by local guards or when a black teenager was shot in Florida showed that there are still gaps. Having a non-white president is not enough. Yet there is no doubt that as compared to 1960, America has made substantial progress in achieving social equality as between whites and blacks. The struggle will continue.

South Africa is another instance which counted as a middle income country in the international income classification. It also had a large share of the state in ownership of means of production. But it was obvious till the final decade of the twentieth century when apartheid was removed that there was no equality of status in South Africa. Here again, while correcting the disadvantages of centuries of discrimination will take time, there is an equality of dignity among the people in the country. There is no doubt that much greater improvement in the life chances of the black population will have to be engineered before juridical equality becomes substantial. Even so, the removal of apartheid is not to be downplayed.

Even in a (racially) more homogenous society such as Britain, there were impediments to equality of dignity for Catholics, non-conformists and Jews till well into the nineteenth century. There is hardly any need to mention the obstacles faced by women. During the second half of the last century, the UK became a multi-racial country. Here again, the presumption of social equality granted by the law has to be supported by political action in delivering substantial equality. There are new dimensions concerning the Roma, for instance, where there is no progress. Equality of respect cannot be taken for granted.

The challenge of equity in India

India adopted a Constitution which established liberal democracy as its norm in political practice with universal adult franchise at its core. But it chose a variant of socialism—Fabian socialism or social democracy as its guiding principle in economic policy. This gave the state a leading role in development. Income equality became a leading concern when it was discovered 10 years after planning was launched that the fruits of development had been shared unequally. The Mahalanobis Committee was appointed to report on this. The details of its report do not concern us except to say that the concern for income equality has remained though not with any discernible impact on actual outcomes.

But while the political framework was revolutionary for a society which had never enjoyed the experience of democracy with a one-person-one-vote system and the economic arrangements had radical pretensions, the decision was made at the advent of independence that social reforms were not to be pursued as part of an official policy. Both the Hindu society and the Muslim one covering the bulk of the population were left to be reformed by private initiatives.[3]

Hindu society is marked by hierarchical divisions in *varna*s and *jati*s. Inequality of status is the guiding principle of the system as Louis Dumont argues; it is also celebrated in his classic study *Homo Hierarchicus* (Dumont 1966/1980). This central social inequality was not addressed by the political classes as they were upper caste. Ambedkar and Nehru made an attempt in the Hindu Code Bill to codify and unify the diverse practices concerning inheritance of property and marriage and women's rights. Even this attempt ran against considerable resistance and had to be pushed piecemeal gently over the years. The Indian political class was found to be socially conservative. This was substantiated when during the 1980s Rajiv Gandhi was prevailed upon to reverse a court judgment in favour of a divorced woman's right to alimony—the Shah Bano affair. The social conservatism of the Indian elite is secular if nothing else.

The mixture of political equality, dirigiste economic development and social conservatism could have proved a lethal combination for the nascent Indian state. B.R. Ambedkar said as much during the closing debates of the Constituent Assembly.

The subsequent evolution of India's political economy, however, has generated an endogenous dynamic to resolving this contradiction. While much remains to be done about achieving social equality as well as reducing income inequality, the phenomenon has been of great interest. It is this that I wish to focus on. This endogenous dynamic has worked through the electoral cycle and democratic contest at the state and the central levels to leverage

---

[3] I have discussed this in my K.R. Narayanan lecture at the Australian National University 'Democracy and Development' (2006).

the numerical strength of the deprived many against the privileged few. This has been called the Mandalization of politics. Its roots go deep into the failure of the economic programme to elevate the conditions of many.

The Nehruvian development paradigm

India's economic development was governed by a drive for national self sufficiency in acquiring its own technology for the production of capital and consumption goods with as little dependence on foreign trade as feasible. The Mahalanobis plan framework was similar to the Feldman plan adopted in the Soviet Union for its planning. This gave priority to Department 1—the capital goods producing sector. The first few decades of planned development thus had a capital intensity bias. It created employment for the highly skilled and educated, working mainly in public sector companies. Employment generation was slow as was the rate of economic growth. For the first 30 years after the initiation of planned growth, gross domestic product (GDP) growth was low relative to the requirements of denting the depth of poverty ; just around 3–3.5 per cent, the so-called Hindu rate of growth. In per capita terms it was just around 1.25 per cent.

The image of the government was that of a socialist progressive government and the pace of growth was thought to be less important than the direction of growth in as much as it was still socialist. Yet the missing dimension of the growth programme was the social profile of the gainers and the losers. The Congress leadership (and indeed that of the Left parties) was upper caste and the beneficiaries were also largely the educated and skilled who were also from the upper castes.[4] As a hegemonic political party, the Congress had an upper caste leadership and a clientelist framework to bring the deprived castes under its umbrella. Even so, the deprived sections

[4] See Christophe Jaffrelot (2010: 459–84) for some background on this issue.

remained behind in the share of gains from growth. This strategy worked for a while but soon it ran into a crisis.[5]

The crisis took the form of the imposition of the Emergency in May 1975 and a suspension of democracy. The immediate background to this step was the judicial case which Prime Minister Indira Gandhi lost. But just the year before there had been anti-inflation protests in Gujarat and Bihar and a nationwide strike by railway workers (employees of a nationalized industry) which was suppressed brutally. These were manifestations of the frustration with slow growth, rampant unemployment and inflation.

The crisis was temporarily resolved when in 1977 the Janata Party, a coalition of anti-Congress forces, came to power. This broke the hegemony of the Congress party and along with it the domination of upper castes in political leadership. One of the important acts of the Janata government was to commission a report on the conditions of social deprivation of a bulk of the population. B.P. Mandal who chaired the commission submitted his report in 1980 (Government of India 1980) but by then the Congress had returned to power. The implementation of the Mandal report had to wait till the second breach in the Congress hegemony when in 1989 it failed to win a majority (and never since has it won a majority on its own).

The commissioning of the Mandal report was a sign of dissatisfaction with the Nehruvian model of development in a bulk of the lower castes. While it may have pursued (albeit unsuccessfully) economic equity with its socialist approach, it had failed to achieve social equality. The upper caste bias of the development model had left the lower castes deprived despite the social democratic and hence radical stance of development.

The report highlighted the strong correlation between *jati* status and economic and social deprivation—the lower the ritual

---

[5] It may be argued that the growth in agriculture, especially during the Green Revolution must have benefited the lower classes. The main beneficiaries were landowners and large tenants. Workers gained due to the opening up of hired labour markets across the states where there was the Green Revolution. But neither poverty numbers nor what came out later under the Mandal report suggests that there was any substantial improvement in the condition of the poor.

jati status the more pronounced the indicators of deprivation. Social inequality had fed the perpetuation of economic inequality. But as growth was slow and the only economic opportunities were concentrated in the public sector, the remedy for relieving social and economic deprivation was seen to be a higher share of public sector jobs for the deprived *jati*s.

Mandalization and the fight for dignity

The implementation of the recommendations of the Mandal Commission led to a lot of political and social unrest. Eventually, however, the principal recommendations were implemented in an augmented fashion. There were reservations not just for jobs in the public sector but also in educational institutions.

The political process which accompanied the implementation of the Mandal recommendations was a true revolution in Indian democracy. The numerically larger lower castes (labelled Other Backward Classes [OBC]) were able to distance themselves from the hegemonic Congress party and form their own regional, *jati*-based coalitional parties whose one-item agenda was advancing the lower classes. In north India—Bihar, Madhya Pradesh, Rajasthan and Uttar Pradesh (the so-called BIMARU states)—the new political formations led by OBC leaders had to initiate policies which corrected several decades, if not centuries, of monopolization of public offices by the upper castes but also to insist on equality of respect from the upper castes (Jaffrelot gives data on how the caste composition of magistrates was changed from upper caste dominance to a much more balanced one with lower caste appointments (Jaffrelot 2010: Table 22.2, p. 476). This took the form of eschewing what was thought to be polite conduct towards the upper castes and insistence on obtaining signs of equal respect from them (south India had a very different social structure as it had gone through an anti-Brahmin political movement in the early twentieth century).

Here the political equality conferred by the democratic process came to the aid of the lower classes. They were able to leverage their numerical superiority via elections into power to alter the rules of the game whereby they could assert their equality of dignity. The hierarchical Hindu caste system legitimized the superiority of the upper castes by standards of ritual purity. Attitudes were deeply embedded in the minds of the lower castes just as much as they were in those of the upper castes. Thus, many lower *jatis* used the strategy of Sanskritization to improve their status. This involved accepting the rules of the hierarchical order and playing within them. The need was for challenging the hierarchical system itself. Breaking this mould required the subversive use of political power by OBC parties.

An important dimension of the use of political power to advance social equity was grasping how ritual inequality fed through opportunities for advancement from early childhood onwards (this is not just an Indian problem. The UK has been exploring changes in nursery education to combat the early privileging of middle class children versus those from a poorer background). Access to education at all levels was unequal between castes. Thus, any merit-based system such as selection on the basis of examination results advantaged the upper castes who had access to higher education and within it, to better institutions. If advantage was unequally distributed due to social inequity and this in turn reinforced economic inequality while leaving social inequity uncorrected, the attack had to be truly radical—on the roots of the system.

Class versus caste

There has always been a debate on the Left of Indian politics as to whether it is class or caste which is the true key to oppression and inequality. The communist parties chose to ignore caste and to emphasize on class. The Congress also took the view that basing policies of affirmative action on the basis of caste would be divisive.[6] This unitarian approach, while seemingly progressive, was one which preserved the hegemony of the elite castes.

---

[6] This was the reason they rejected the recommendations of the first (Kalelkar) Commission on Backward Classes which reported in the 1950s.

The Marxian notion of class is based on the position of a group with respect to the means of production. While this puts production as central to a social analysis, it ignores the myriad other activities which determine the human as well as material resources available to a member of any class. Access to education, barriers to mobility and discrimination in employment are important dimensions in determining the economic status of members of a class and are crucial in reproducing social relations. A narrow interpretation of class neglects these aspects.

Ram Manohar Lohia was one person who insisted on treating caste as a fundamental obstacle to equality in Indian society. He proved to be one political thinker/leader with the deepest impact on Indian democracy. He saw the centrality of the need to dismantle the hierarchical system of caste. It was perhaps his training in Germany as a philosopher which led him to such an original stance. It is also remarkable that both Lohia and Jai Prakash Narayan were from Bihar. Perhaps it was the widespread and historically deep experience of Buddhism in Bihar which made them alive to the evils of the caste system since Buddha rejected the *varna* system.

From social to economic equity

Whatever the origins of the idea of rejecting caste, its practical impact was in empowering lower *jati*s to use the ballot box to alleviate their social status. Leaders such as Lalu Prasad Yadav and Mulayam Singh Yadav neglected all other issues of governance to concentrate on the dignity agenda. This has proved to be an ineffective strategy for the long run because of both historical and modern circumstances.

Historically, the Hindu society has maintained its cohesion by dividing the people in strictly ranked cellular divisions of *jati*s with an overarching role for the apex caste of Brahmins. This held society together despite the absence of any Hindu kingship which commanded authority over the entire territory. The cellular divisions prevented the lower *jati*s from getting together to challenge the hegemony of the upper castes. Thus, even while the OBCs united temporarily after the Mandal report, soon there were divisions and the articulations of Most Backward Classes and others, which fragmented the OBC coalition. Hence, rival parties grew up to represent the case of sections among the OBCs while the traditional elite parties also found ways of co-opting many *jatis* and offering them much more than they used to.

This division had a healthy rather than an adverse effect. Social equality was a necessary condition for basic equality but the need for economic advancement remained urgent as ever. Thus, regional parties had to deliver economic betterment if they wanted to retain power. In Bihar the changeover from Lalu Prasad Yadav's Rashtriya Janata Dal (RJD) to Nitish Kumar's Janata Dal (United) (JDU) as the ruling party demonstrated this transition.

Lalu Prasad Yadav openly asserted that he wanted respect not development (*vikas nahi samman chahiye*). So while he achieved a lot for the status of OBCs socially he failed to register any income or employment growth in Bihar. Nitish Kumar represented the Kurmis, a numerically smaller *jati* in Bihar than the Yadavs. He pursued a development strategy which benefited a larger section of the Bihar population.[7]

The struggle for social equity is seldom fully over. The example of women's fight for equality of dignity across the world illustrates this. Yet the achievement of social equity also has a dialectical effect on the advancement of economic equity. First effects of achieving equal status for groups previously regarded as lower, are often to make them assertive and economically less productive than before. This paradoxical outcome was observed, for example, during the reconstruction period in the US. Following the Civil War, the social position of black Americans improved suddenly but at the same time there were reports of economic inefficiency and deterioration in incomes (some of these reports may have been biased). There are also frequent accounts of postcolonial nations suffering a temporary deterioration in the economic dimension on gaining independence. Thus, often the immediate effect of the

---

[7] I have discussed this in 'Efficiency, Governance and Growth' *in The New Bihar* (2013).

gain in social equity is adverse on economic efficiency. The rise in the status of OBCs who were often exploited as landless workers (or casual labourers owning small pieces of land) led them to work less hard and productivity suffered. The growth rate of state GDP slowed down during the years of RJD rule.

Such adverse effects are temporary and can be reversed by supplementing the policy for social equity by larger investments in human capital—health and education of the workers, for example. This is what seems to have happened in Bihar after 2005. There was sustained investment in infrastructure, agriculture as well as in human capital. The complex process of this dialectical interaction between social and economic equity remains to be investigated in detail.[8]

Conclusion

Social equity is an important but often ignored dimension of inclusive development. It should be primary to economic equity but is often presumed to be a given. The interplay between the two notions of social and economic equity needs more study. This is just a beginning.

References

Desai, Meghnad. (2002). *Marx's Revenge: The Resurgence of Capitalism and the Death of Statist Socialism*. London: Verso.
——— .(2006). *Development and Nationhood: Essays in South Asian Political Economy*. New Delhi: Oxford University Press.
———. (2013). 'Efficiency, Governance and Growth: Understanding the Bihar Experience', in N.K. Singh and N. Stern (eds), *The New Bihar*. New Delhi: Harper and Collins.
Dumont, Louis. (1966/1980). *Homo Hierarchicus* (French original translated in 1980). Chicago IL: University of Chicago Press.

---

[8] See *Efficiency, Governance and Growth* (2013) for a formal model of the interaction.

Government of India. (1980). *Report of the Backward Classes Commission in 2 Volumes.* New Delhi: Government of India.

Jaffrelot, Christophe. (2010). *Religion, Caste and Politics in India.* Delhi: Primus Books.

Rawls, John. (1971). *A Theory of Justice.* Cambridge MA: Harvard University Press.

Chapter 3

Beyond 'Cleavage Politics'

Dipankar Gupta

Limits of cleavage politics

Take a look at the agitations around the world and feel good that we are indeed part of the global order. Not only have the Tweeterati and the internet altered ways of communicating political activism, but the phenomenon itself has also undergone a change both internationally and in India too.

In the past it was class against class, producers against non-producers, grain growers versus revenue appropriators, rich migrants versus poor autochthones and so on. In short, democracy thrived on 'cleavage politics' when activism depended on the economy's faultlines to energize itself (Lipset and Rokkan 1967). These then formed the natural political territories of different parties and that is what gave them stability. Nationalism and industrialization produced the further separation between those at the Centre and marginal groups at the peripheries as well as the enduring tensions between economic classes.

Even when distances seemed to be clearly cultural in flavour and form, they easily lent themselves to economic livelihood markers. These drew sustenance from the location that people held with respect to the factors of production—land, labour, capital, enterprise. It would, therefore, be appropriate to term these prime movers of social mobilization to be 'factor producerist' in character. If migrants were brutalized by the 'sons of the soil' the deep answer should be sought in the realm of economic differences.

Castes were also seen in factor producerist (or, simply, producerist) terms—landlord against tenants, manual workers against mental workers, cultivators versus artisans, to name a few binaries. Gender differences too were understood along similar lines. It was crucial to know who works indoors and who works outside, who milks the cow and who trains the ox. What was generally common in these 'producerist' themes was that some people had fatter wallets to beat up others with.

Not anymore: politics now trumps economics, and it has done that repeatedly on the streets and squares of India in the near past. The most energetic political expressions in recent times in India were the anti-corruption movement of 2011, the unrest in the aftermath of the brutal rape in December 2012 and closer up, the rise of the Aam Aadmi Party in 2013. In these instances the troops did not rally around social cleavages, or faultlines that separated classes, communities or estates, but were prompted by the call of citizenship.

More specifically, the outcry in Delhi and in other urban centres (not all large, as with the Anna Hazare 2011 mobilization) was to hold the government responsible for poor delivery of civic services. It was not as if this was a recent complaint, but as the activists said, and large numbers happily acquiesced, misrule had now reached a crescendo. Corruption and political high-handedness were seen as the principal factors behind the popular, public anger against the party in power and this resentment was not limited to any one class, or gender. It was a united front, of sorts, where multiple classes, rural and urban, the highly educated and the not so well lettered, came together to demand, as citizens, services from the state.

Instead of the old political categories around cleavages based on one's location in 'factor producerist' terms, we now have the emergence of 'citizen consumerism'. In this emerging altered political format the demands are for services that are promised as part of the democratic contract between citizens and the state. This is what has stunned established political parties because they were still playing with cleavages and hanging on to old ghosts that were indeed very scary once.

In essential terms, this phenomenon is also reflected in the 'Arab Spring' uprising; in what happened in Brazil in 2013 around the construction of a football stadium; in Istanbul 2013 when the government decided to concretize a park and build a mall on it; and, indeed, in what is going on today in the anti-graft and pro-democracy agitations in Thailand. Categories drawn from factor producerist categories are not only of little relevance in comprehending these political mobilizations, but they may well be misleading too. In all such mobilizations, there is little doubt that *civic consumerism* is what gave them their appeal and diacritic. As a result, producerist ideologies that build on economic themes are struggling to be heard. Perhaps, their day will return, but it is clearly not in the immediate future.

The double barreled term 'civic consumerism' should not be confused with the more widely known term, 'consumerism'. The latter denotes an unending greed to buy the latest and aggrandize oneself with possessions that have a built-in obsolescent element in them. The 'consumerists', however, are those who demand services from the state and society in order to realize ambitions that help them move beyond their initial status. 'Consumerists' operate from different starting points just as pure consumers do. But unlike consumerism, in the 'civic consumerist' urge, the state comes before the market.

It is not as if factories in India, or even the Asia–Pacific region, are today humming the sweet sounds of contentment (see Macdonald 1997: 13), and yet industrial unrest around 'factor producerist' demands are becoming increasingly rare. Notwithstanding the recent Maruti strike near Delhi, rarely do we see a full-throated movement of the farmers or of the workers where the 'producerist' theme is centralized. In fact, the number of strikes has fallen significantly. As recently as in 1979, there were 3,187 strikes and lockouts in India, but by 2000 the number had come down to 771 and in 2006 it was a low 346 (www.theopendata.com/site/2012/03/ strikes-and-lockouts-in-India/; accessed on 20 January 2013, and www.industrialrelations.naukrihub.com/analyses-of-strikes.html; accessed on 22 January 2013).

Misreading civic consumerism as factor producerism

We should, as always, begin with what is most obvious. There is no doubt that the anti-corruption movement or the public outrage against rape, have brought people together, across class and 'producerist' categories, like never before. As these participants do not come with specific working class, rural or white collar interests, they are often viewed with cynicism. If the protesters appear rootless then that aspect should be centralized and not marginalized in our study of contemporary India.

We are so used to 'producerist' grooves that anything that defeats them, or ignores them makes us intellectually very uncomfortable. That civic consumerism is what drives people to politics can also be gauged from the fact that when established political parties lead demonstrations against price rise or foreign direct investment (FDI) in retail they look so stagey and contrived. The popular passion to buoy them is missing because the old 'producerist' commitment and clarity are no longer there. Unless civic consumerist issues are in the spotlight, popular endorsements will be hard to get.

The recent 2013 elections in Delhi can act as a pointer in this connection. What mattered most to the electorate were issues of corruption, the high electricity rates, privileges and perks of those in high office and inflation. None of these issues is class-specific, except that it affects different classes with differing degrees of severity. The election results clearly show that except for those at the rarefied top, everybody else is negotiating through the system in *bad, bad faith*. Earlier cleavages such as between rural and urban, or between workers and capitalists, or even between castes, no longer heat politics the way they used to.

In fact, when was caste last heard of in election campaigns over the past five years, or so? The Bharatiya Janata Party (BJP) has junked the Hindu–Muslim divide; the Badals in Punjab rarely recall the Panth; and Akhilesh Yadav in Uttar Pradesh dishes out computer tablets and not caste war. There are good reasons for these changes to happen. Rural–urban distinctions are not that clear anymore, nor do caste ties lock people into the ways of the past. This is why aspirations converge across the country, regardless of class and community.

Everywhere, and for everybody, the road to the future is via education, health and civic services. As a result, political leaders are now forced to compete against one another in expressing this social urge rather than pitting those on one side of a social cleavage against the other. Dividing voters along old faultlines was once as easy as parting one's hair, but not any longer. To a significant extent then, it is now a question of how political parties address collective aspirations rather than sectional causes.

Experts have yet to wise up, but election previews show that flaunting cleavage in politics does not work that well anymore. Citizens are beginning to vault across social faults to unitedly press for a dignified delivery of civic consumerist services from governments of the day. This trend has every potentiality of growing in the years to come.

Urbanization and the emergence of civic consumerism

Where did the forces that undermined the 'producerist' logic emanate from? What has happened in the years between 1980 till now that warrant a fresh examination of reality as well as the conceptual tools to apprehend it? We did not see a revolution, any major convulsion, or any clear breakdown of our society, so why has 'producerism' lost out? Surely, no one conceptual system will get it right all the time, but why is 'producerism' so clearly out of step with what is happening on the streets? Political parties seem unable, or just unwilling, to accept this change, for it hurts certain vital interest groups in them. This, however, is not a burden sociology carries and it can, therefore, undertake such an enquiry without inhibitions.

If producerism has lost its symbolic energy, there are good reasons for this. The most important one, however, is the breakdown of the village economy and the growing rates of urbanization. As urbanization in India, Tunisia or Egypt is unaccompanied by adequate social services and delivery mechanisms, civic anger against the governments of the day has grown. It is urbanization without social buffers which is the new melting pot. It is this that is making a hash of old 'producerist' categories and is uniting under-served citizens instead.

Look at the urban profile of some of these countries that are now heaving with 'civic consumerist' anger. Brazil today is nearly 85 per cent urban, but was only 46 per cent urban in 1960. Tunisia, likewise, is today 66 per cent urban, a jump of nearly 30 per cent from what it was in 1960. Cairo houses 25 per cent of Egypt's entire population and half of the country's urban population and Bangkok is home to over 30 per cent of Thais. Now take a look at India. In the past 10 years, there were 18 new million plus cities in India, 72 new Class I towns and over 2,770 new census towns (Government of India 2011). For the first time, the increase in the urban population in actual numbers and not percentages, has exceeded that of the rural population. A closer examination will also tell us that in every village there is a town waiting to come out. Both country and town have been gradually moulded by these pressures and have assumed visages that would have been quite unrecognizable in the past.

Consequently, it is no longer easy to distinguish between industrial and non-industrial workers, between rural and urban occupations and between residence in village and city. With the coming of liberalization, some of the earlier tendencies such as pressure on agriculture, have become more tangible. At the same time, with the emergence of the export sector, a large part of the rural workforce has moved quite spontaneously to non-farm occupations. Thus, while their educational levels and skill sets have not changed by much, their locations, both at home and at work, have altered a great deal.

Today, roughly 93 per cent of our workforce is in the informal sector. In fact, between 1999 and 2004 the proportion of informal labour employed in the formal sector went up from roughly 36 to 45 per cent. Farmers are no longer just farmers, even if, as industry and factory workers, they have recently turned earth in their fingernails. Agriculturists and labour constitute the bulk of our population and the boundaries between them are getting blurred.

When we come to the white collar class, including those with frayed white collars, many of them are barely hanging in. Conversations around their dinner tables are not always pleasurable, nor the fare on it appetizing. An illness, a death and an ambition to study further, can put tremendous pressure on such families. This is why many of those who gathered at Anna Hazare's rally in 2011, and joined the anti-rape agitations in 2012, came from angry, middle class to almost middle class backgrounds.

Many of the young among them had pieces of paper that showed off their degrees or diplomas but who were either unemployed or employed below their perceived station. Some of them were a few generations urban, others still had home and family in villages, yet their enemies were not sectorized in different 'producerist' categories like landlord or capitalist. Instead, they had a common enemy and they saw its face in the undelivering state.

How did we get here? Let us start with rural India.

Why the 'rural' is not really rural anymore

India was long considered to be an agricultural society, but not anymore. When India became a free country, almost 50 per cent of the economy was dependent on agriculture; today it barely contributes 13.9 per cent to our national economy. The rate of growth in agriculture also hovers around 2.5 to 3.5 per cent per annum. This, as we can easily tell, is well below the GDP growth figures for the country as a whole.

Much of this transformation has been credited to land reforms but, if anything, this policy has worked largely in absentia. After some initial breakthrough in the 1950s and 1960s, it did precious little to alter the rural landscape. Demography and population rise took over at this point, sub-divided holdings within generations and accomplishing what land reforms were meant to. Consequently, about 80 per cent of farms today are below five acres and about 66 per cent are below three acres. Not surprisingly, most of them are family run where hired labour hardly figures, except perhaps during the peak harvesting season. This is why the numbers of large and even medium farmers are shrinking while those of small and marginal farmers keep growing (Ministry of Agriculture 2003; see also http://dacnet.nic.in; accessed on 4 March 2011; Chand et al. 2011: 7; Government of India, 2006).

That this has been happening steadily over the years does not lessen the effect of its cumulative impact on agriculture. All of this indicates that the categories with which we viewed the countryside are not relevant anymore. What is also true is that there is little reluctance towards acknowledging this reality on the part of those who encounter such category blurs. Naturally, therefore, the earlier understanding of rural India needs to be revisited and, perhaps, abandoned.

By now agriculturists are ready to accept the fact that their future lies elsewhere, perhaps in cities and towns, perhaps also in household and informal industries. If they cannot make it to those places, at least their children should. Thus, while cultivators, in general, constitute about 44 per cent of the rural population, this number rises to 63.6 per cent if we take only those among them who are over 60 years of age (*Manpower Profile of India* 2009: 233). Most small family farms are clearly being tended to by the older generation so that their young can go out into the big, wide world.

No wonder then that the hallowed and long-cherished cleavage between urban and rural is facing rough weather. Many of our villages will not qualify as rural if the official definition that 75 per cent of working age males should be attached to agriculture is followed. Very often people continue to live and work in villages but are almost urban in terms of their occupational profiles. So the earlier line that separated a farmer from a worker is slowly getting erased as well.

As a result there has been a tremendous increase in Rural Non-Farm Employment (RNFE) all over the country. What was once a secondary occupation for most villagers is often the primary one today. The National Sample Survey (66th Round) shows that the percentage of non-agricultural households increased from a pre-existing high of 31.9 per cent in 1993–94 to 42.5 per cent in 2009–10 (*National Sample Survey* 2010; see also http://www.indiastat.com/india/showdata.asp?secid=324; accessed on 7 August 2013).

What is equally noteworthy is that the rural non-farm sector contributes as much as 45.5% of rural net domestic product (http://www.indiastat.com: 58; see also Chaddha 2003: 55). Nor is this a story of the backward regions in India. In fact, the more backward the districts, the higher the proportion of men in household industries. In Uttar Pradesh (UP), for example, six times more men than women work in these manufactories and in Rajasthan the figure jumps to an unbelievable 10 (Government of India, *Census of India* 2001: Part [II] B 9i] Primary Census Abstract: General Population).

There has also been a steady rise in the migration of male workers from rural to urban India. In less than 10 years, from 1999–2000 to 2007–08, the number went up from 36.5 to 41.6 per cent (see Kundu and Saraswati 2012: 221). In just one year, between 1999 and 2000, the proportion of people migrating for jobs jumped by as much as 15 per cent (*Manpower Profile of India* 2005: 303, Table 6.12).

It is, therefore, legitimate to conclude that in recent years, impressive mobility notwithstanding, the poor have moved nearly always as informal labour. All of this goes to show that we need to check if the diacritics that once served so well in separating town from country are relevant any longer. It should not be surprising then that over 5 billion railway tickets are sold every year in India. As anyone who knows this country will vouch that even this figure is an understatement for most people travel ticketless on the Indian Railways.

Horizontal mobility and aspirations

All of this may have led to greater 'producerist' resistance if the opportunities for switching jobs and residence were not there. This is an imponderable 'if' and need not detain us just yet. That the poor could move from poverty to poverty with a change of locale also meant a release of hope and a certain disdain for going back to where they once were. These migrants, poorly trained and desperate for work, will do anything for a living (Kundu and Mohanan 2010).

If these rural migrants have been absorbed to some extent in non-agricultural jobs it is because, in India, surprisingly skilled labour is not in high demand in industrial occupations either. This is where 'globalization' and its cohort 'economic liberalization' have played a role. In particular, one should emphasize the significance that the opening of the export sector after the 1991 economic reforms has had on social relations. It is this that has undone many of the earlier 'producerist' categories that had held for decades. It is this again that has allowed horizontal, if not always vertical, mobility for those looking for alternatives to a rural life but without too many skills in the bag.

India's growth story thus requires a full acknowledgment of the contributions of the small-scale sector and of informal labour to our export earnings. From textiles to gems and jewellery to shelling cashew nuts, workers in these industries contribute enormously to our foreign earnings. In 2005–06, gems and jewellery exports from India constituted 15 per cent of its total merchandise export, but also 8 per cent of the world trade. Lowly carpet weaving that takes place in little mud huts in districts like Jaunpur and Mirzapur in east Uttar Pradesh actually make for as much as 11 per cent of the global demand for floor coverings (*Economic Survey* 2006–07: p-S 118, Table 6.8).

Poor as they are, they are connected to the world market. Perhaps, it is because they are poor that the buyers outside are interested in what they produce. Employing cheap labour is the Indian way of edging out international competition. In this process, as we have noted, several good (read formal) industries have gone bad (National Commission for Enterprises in the Unorganized Sector 2007). After the violent 2012 strike, the Maruti management grudgingly acknowledged that it had erred in increasing the number of contract labour, at the expense of regular ones, inside their factory gates.

Horizontal mobility and the demise of old statuses meant the release of new ambitions and in new surroundings. Now education has assumed much greater importance for the poor for they see it as a reliable way of edging out poverty and, for many, this has also resulted in upward mobility. For most, however, the piece of paper that they call a 'degree' or a 'diploma' is not getting them a job. They know enough English to realize that their English is not good enough; they have enough contacts in the world to know that their contacts are not good enough either.

Health services, too, are more critical today because nobody can be ill for too long as wages are paid by the day, if not by the hour. Besides, when there are available health technologies, it is hurtful and tragic if they are denied to some because they are expensive. Hence, families go into debt very quickly if somebody falls seriously ill. The out-of-pocket expenditure on health is roughly 78 per cent (see Shiva Kumar et al. 2010), which is just about the highest in the world along with Pakistan and Afghanistan. According to one estimate, 39 million people are dunked yearly below the poverty line for medical reasons (Sinha 2011; see also Shiva Kumar et al. 2010).

Education expenses consume poor households and they pay for this far more than what they can afford. Given the miserable performance of government teachers, enrolment in private schools has gone up phenomenally. In the 1980s merely 2 per cent of the country's children were in private schools. Today the numbers have ballooned. About 21 per cent of the children are enrolled in private schools in rural India and this figure goes up to 51 per cent when we come to the urban population (Desai et al. 2010: 82).

Even among the lowest income quintile as many as 15 per cent of the children go to private schools (Desai et al. 2010: 82). Yet, so far education has not quite yielded the benefits that were expected of it. For example, Uma Rani shows with the help of her field notes, that that roughly 58 per cent have a secondary or a higher secondary school degree (Rani 2008: 698). So a school education, which is hard fought, does not take the poor very far.

That is how disillusioning government schools are! Therefore, if one still insists on education for the poor along the old format, this will end up as poor education. In the past, this may not have worried impoverished villagers as much, but it does now. Yet, so far education has not quite yielded the benefits that were expected of it. For example, Uma Rani's field study shows that among the unskilled labour force, roughly 58 per cent of the unskilled labour force had a secondary or a higher secondary school degree (Rani 2008: 698). So a school education is not always what it is cut out to be—not, at least, in terms of eventual outcomes.

In the health sector again, the story is similar. There is a great distrust towards government hospitals and dispensaries though they are present in the countryside. As people now must get well quick, because their impermanent jobs depend on it, they rush to private doctors where the treatment is more expensive than the government option. Though 86 per cent of government doctors have a proper degree as compared to only 60 per cent among private practitioners (Desai et al. 2010: 106), yet 66 per cent, most of them poor, seek non-state medical help (Indian Human Development Report 2011: 169).

It is hardly surprising why this should be so. Health expenditure is less than 1 per cent of our GDP and education less than 3 per cent. By all standards, these sums are very low. In other upper middle income countries, for example, 3.4 per cent of GDP is devoted to health (Gupta 2002: 54). Government services, including those of the doctor, as well as the school master (whom we encountered earlier) provide dreadful services. Consequently, a significant number of people fall into chronic debt every year on account of medical expenses.

If we take just education and health, then there is very little reason to cheer. Much more than any time in the past does the woeful delivery of these services hurt so much today. Liberalization has let loose the market, but it has also released ambitions that need services to back them up. Except for some 2.6 million employed by the central government and about 7.2 million by different states, only the very rich can be sanguine about healthcare in India.

Our inability to provide for both health and education is certainly not because we do not have the money. More than the amount of resources we spend on these subjects, it is also the mechanism of state delivery that counts. This is where the citizens' 'civic consumerist' urges are left unsatisfied. They feel they are entitled to state services but are short-changed all the way by the ruse of targeted policies which only attract corrupt politicians and bureaucrats. Which is why when the government talks about the money it has spent on health and education, the first question that comes up among the citizens is: what about delivery?

Thus, while we may boast of the fact that we have a large number of primary schools and primary health centres, the actual availability of these services is well below par. Take another random example: so many households are said to be electrified, yet only 6 per cent of these have regular power and another 26 per cent for less than 12 hours a day (Desai et al. 2010: 65). In all of this, citizens, as consumers of state services, feel turned down, time and again. No wonder, the ire of the public today is focused on the state and has shifted from other antagonistic 'producerist' categories, as was the case till not too long ago.

The citizens' front and civic consumerism

Social welfare services, from health to education to security and housing are essentials of civic consumerism. As these affect all classes, it creates a demand for civic consumerism that is not cleavage based. If any of these services are docketed specially for certain target groups, like the poor, or the Scheduled Castes, they will only attract corruption. We have a long history of this beginning with Antyodaya Anna Yojana to Mahatma Gandhi National Rural Employment Guarantee Act (MNREGA). When governments rely on such emblematic gestures they only succeed in miring our society in a low-wage economy which, in the not-so-long-run will affect the rich adversely too.

When it comes to societal well-being, the rich cannot do it by themselves. They cannot reproduce talents endogenously, nor can they buy their way to everything. They cannot escape pollution or dengue, nor can they get state-of-the-art health and education when the general standards in these sectors are falling all over. Where will the talent for good doctors and teachers come from if a bulk of the population is locked in poor schools and hospitals? As a result, India has only six physicians per 10,000 population, whereas China, no leader in the field of health, has 14 (Indian Human Development Report 2011:166).

Not every teacher or doctor can hope to go abroad, or get a happy position in a private hospital or school. This will obviously deprive these sectors of a regular flow of talent that draws on a wide social base. Consequently, to be a doctor or an engineer or a teacher may not be quite as starry an option as it once was. This will drive the costs for these services in the private sector even higher and the standards of training and delivery at the state levels even lower. That is how closely the worlds of the rich and the poor are connected through the medium of social services.

The most intellectually challenging projects for the future will not be between this or that 'producerist' category, such as class or status groups, as it has been for a long time. The future that suggests itself to us will test academics to examine and explain how state services reach out to citizens and how citizens view the state. No doubt, these issues will be refracted through categories, but they will not be dominated by those of 'producerist' provenance. In such endeavours, the state will be the common point of reference and this will often merge differences between people on several issues. While the citizens are not, and will not be, a homogeneous mass, yet the attention of its different constituents will be largely on the delivery of state services. As a result, the unities between citizens will be much greater than what has been in the past.

References

Chaddha, G.K. (2003). 'Rural Non Farm Sector in the Indian Economy: Growth, Challenges and Future Direction' (mimeo), paper presented in the joint Jawaharlal Nehru University and IFPRI Workshop, 'The Dragon and the Elephant: A Comparative Study of Economic Reforms in China and India', 25–26 March, New Delhi.

Chand, Ramesh, P.A. Lakshmi Prasanna, Aruna Singh. (2011). 'Farm Size and Productivity: Understanding the Strength of Small Holders and Improving their Livelihoods', *Economic and Political Weekly* XLVI (26–27): 5–11.

Desai, Sonade. et al. (2010). *Human Development in India: Challenges for a Society in Transition.* New Delhi: Oxford University Press.

Government of India (2001). *Census of India 2001.* New Delhi: Registrar General of Census, Government of India.

———. (2006). *National Sample Survey* 2006: *Some Aspects of Operational Land Holdings in India, 2002–03.* New Delhi: National Sample Survey Organisation, Ministry of Statistics and Implementation, Government of India.

———. (2006–07). *Economic Survey 2005–06.* New Delhi: Ministry of Finance and Economic Division, Government of India

———. (2010). *National Sample Survey 2010: Employment and Unemployment Situation in India,* Report Number 537. New Delhi: Ministry of Statistics and Implementation, Government of India.

———. (2011). *Census of India 2011.* Available at: censusofindia. gov.in/2011prov-results/paper2/data_files/India2/1.%20 Data%Highlight.pdf; accessed on 15 March 2014.

Gupta, S.P. (2002). *Report on the Committee on India Vision 2020.* New Delhi: Planning Commission, Government of India.

Indian Human Development Report. (2011). Sonalde Desai, Amaresh Dubey, Brij Raj Joshi, Mitali Sen, Abusaleh Shariff and Reeve Vanneman (eds). *Indian Human Development Report 2011.* New Delhi: Oxford University Press

Institute of Applied Manpower Research. (2005). *Manpower Profile of India.* New Delhi: Concept Publishing House.

Institute of Applied Manpower Research. (2009). *Manpower Profile of India.* New Delhi: Concept Publishing House.

Kundu, Amitabh and P.C. Mohanan. (2010). 'Employment and Inequality Outcomes in India'. Available at: http://www.oecd.org/ dataoecd/54/51/42546020.pdf; accessed on 23 December 2010.

Kundu, Amitabh and Lopamudra Ray Saraswati. (2012). 'Migration and Exclusionary Urbanization in India', *Economic and Political Weekly*, XLVII (26–27): 212–27.

Lipset, Seymour Martin and Stein Rokkan. (1967). 'Cleavage Structure, Party Systems and Voter Alignments: Introduction', in Seymour Martin Lipset and S. Rokkan (eds), *Party Systems and Voter Alignments: Cross National Perspectives*. New York: Free Press-Collier-Macmillan.

Macdonald, David. (1997). 'Industrial Relations and Globalization', paper presented in ILO ACT/EMP Workshop in Turin, Italy, 15 May.

National Commission for Enterprises in the Unorganised Sector. (2007). *Report on Conditions of Work and Promotion of Livelihoods in the Unorganised Sector*. New Delhi: NCEUP.

Rani, Uma. (2008). 'Leaving Workshops: Informal Processes of Learning and Skill Acquisition in Auto Component Firms Supplying to Global Production Networks', in J. Unni and Uma Rani (eds), *Flexibility of Labour in Globalizing Economies: The Challenge of Skill and Technology*. New Delhi: Tulika Books, p. 102.

Shiva Kumar, A.K. Lincoln Chen, Mita Choudhury, Vijay Mahajan, Amarjeet Sinha. (2010). 'Framing Health Care: Challenges and Opportunities', *The Lancet*, 37 (9766): 668–79.

Sinha, Koutelya. (2011). 'Indians Pay 78% of their Medical Expenses from their own Pocket', The *Times of India*, 13 January.

Chapter 4

What do the Voters Reward?

Poonam Gupta *

Introduction

Election results are usually hard to predict. India is no exception. Even as the question of what the voters care about while casting their votes has remained of perennial interest to academics and politicians themselves, election results have become particularly unpredictable in India in the last two decades due to the decline of single-party dominance.

In principle, any number of factors may influence a voter's decision. These include the personal attributes of the candidates— gender, education, appearance; their party affiliations; caste or religious identity of the voters and the candidates; and finally, for a more discerning voter, the performance of the candidate, or that of the party may matter as well.

* This article is based on the author's joint work with Professor Arvind Panagariya and Professor Bhaskar Dutta when she was working at the National Institute of Public Finance and Policy, Delhi. Comments are welcome at pgupta. nipfp@gmail.com.

In this essay, we look at the factors which explain election results, using the data for the 2009 parliamentary elections. We use the candidate-level information for the analysis. A landmark judgment of the Supreme Court in 2002 required every candidate contesting state and national elections to submit a legal affidavit disclosing his educational qualifications, information about his personal wealth and importantly, any criminal cases against him or her. The court also stipulated that wide publicity should be given to the contents of the affidavits so that the electorate could take an informed decision about whom to elect as their legislators. We collected this data, as well as the data on the economic performance under incumbent parties in states to look at the effect of factors related to a candidate's characteristics, his or her party affiliation or the incumbent's performance on the voting outcome.[1]

Our results show that party affiliation and the performance of the party at the state level were significant factors in determining electoral outcomes. In particular, the economic performance of the state under the incumbent party dwarfed all other factors in importance. After controlling for affiliation with a large party or the incumbents' performance, only a few of a candidate's characteristics were important in influencing the outcome. Among candidate characteristics, education, age, and most importantly, wealth affected the vote share that each candidate got. Wealthier and more educated candidates got a larger vote share. Wealth is important in explaining why even candidates facing criminal charges fare well in elections.

The rest of the essay is organized as follows: in the next section, we briefly discuss recent trends in elections, specifically the results of the 2009 elections. We then analyse which of the personal, party or performance factors mattered in explaining the election outcomes in 2009. The section that follows looks at the factors affecting the electoral prospects of candidates with criminal charges against them in particular. The last section offers a conclusion.

---

[1] We derive the data on these variables directly from the Election Commission's website as well as from a website maintained by the Association for Democratic Reforms (ADR), http://myneta.info.

Details of the 2009 parliamentary elections

Outcomes in Indian elections have become increasingly fragmented. As can be seen in Figure 4.1, the number of parties, which have at least one member in the Lok Sabha has increased over time, the largest jump occurring in 1998. Thus, in recent years, the formation of a government has required a coalition of several parties, and as a result the smaller parties with just a handful of Members of Parliament (MPs) have come to wield considerable power.

India has more than a 1,000 registered political parties. These are divided into national, state and unrecognized parties. Any registered party that lacks the status of a state or a national party is an unrecognized party. The Election Commission confers the status of a state party on any party that meets certain thresholds in terms of votes received and seats won in an election. A state party acquires a monopoly on the use of its party symbol in the state. A party qualifying as a state party in four states gets a national status and then has the monopoly over the use of its election symbol over the entire country. It is not unusual for parties to lose their 'national' status once they lose the qualifications for it.

Table 4.1 gives the broad results of the elections held in 1999, 2004 and 2009. It shows that the national parties numbering six or more won only a little more than two-thirds of the seats in each of the three elections. Unsurprisingly, in the context, the party

Figure 4.1 Number of parties with at least one Member of Parliament in the Lok Sabha

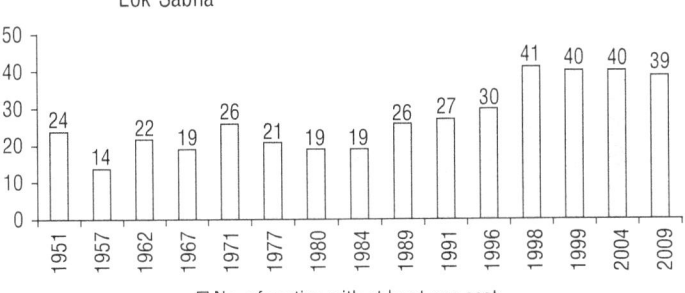

□ No. of parties with at least one seat

Source: Author's own calculations.

Table 4.1 Results of the elections in 1999, 2004 and 2009

(Number of seats won by various parties in each election)

Party		1999	2004	2009
National Parties	Total seats	369	364	376
	Indian National Congress	114	145	206
	Bharatiya Janata Party	182	138	116
	Bahujan Samaj Party	14	19	21
	Nationalist Congress Party		9	9
	Communist Party of India	4	10	4
	Communist Party of India (Marxist)	33	43	16
	Rashtriya Janata Dal		24	4
State Parties	Total seats	158	159	146
	Samajwadi Party		36	23
	Janata Dal (U)		8	20
	All India Trinamool Congress		2	19
	DMK		16	18
	Biju Janata Dal		11	14
	Shiv Sena		12	11
	AIADMK		0	9
	Telugu Desam Party		5	6
	Janata Dal (S)		4	3
Other (unrecognized) parties		10	15	12
Independent candidates		6	5	9
Total		543	543	543

Source: Compiled by the author, based on the data obtained from the Election Commission's website.

winning the largest number of seats has fallen well short of a majority so that each government has been based on a multi-party coalition. Because the party with the second most seats ends up in the opposition, state parties, which together account for approximately 30 per cent of the seats have come to acquire great power.

Results in the last two elections in particular have defied most post-poll projections and have produced surprising results. Led by the Bharatiya Janata Party (BJP), the National Democratic Alliance (NDA) ruled India from 1999 to 2004. But, the BJP suffered major losses, shrinking its seats from 182 to 138 in the 2004 elections, whereas the Congress party improved its score significantly from 114 to 145 seats, though it was still well short of the 272 seats necessary to form a government. But remarkably, it was successful in cobbling together a coalition that came to be known as the United Progressive Alliance (UPA). The UPA government successfully served its full term until 2009. The 2009 national elections yielded a result that was different from the 2004 elections: it returned the main ruling party, the Congress party to power with a larger number of seats as well as with a larger victory margin. Beating even the most optimistic predictions, the Congress increased its tally from 145 to an impressive 206 seats. The Marxist Communist Party suffered the worst losses, shrinking from 43 to 16 seats. The BJP also declined from 138 to 116 seats. Thus, between 1999 and 2009, the Congress and the BJP had more or less exchanged their positions. How can one explain the relative performance of the Congress party in 2009? We come back to this later in the essay.

Some details about the 2009 elections include: 8,071 candidates contested the elections. Of these, 3,825 or 47.4 per cent were candidates with no party affiliations, that is, they contested as independents; 30 per cent of the candidates were affiliated to national or regional parties and the rest belonged to unrecognized parties. In all, 372 parties fielded one or more candidates. The average number of candidates per constituency was 15 with the maximum and minimum number of candidates in any constituency being 43 and three respectively. Remarkably, as the latter figure indicates, there was not a single constituency with a direct contest between two candidates. Countrywide, 59.4 per cent of the voters voted. The maximum turnout was 90.4 per cent (in the Tamluk constituency in West Bengal) and the minimum was 25.6 per cent (in the Srinagar constituency in Jammu and Kashmir). The top four candidates in each constituency accounted for more than 90 per cent of the total votes polled.

Party affiliations in general, and affiliation to a national or state party in particular, played a crucial role in determining outcomes: candidates with a party affiliation accounted for more than 98 per cent of the top four candidates and for a majority of the winning candidates. Only nine winning candidates contested as independents, while the 534 winning candidates out of a maximum possible of 543 had some party affiliation.

What matters in elections: Personal characteristics, party or performance?

Candidate characteristics: A typical candidate/winner in Lok Sabha elections 2009[2]

Contrary to popular belief, Lok Sabha members enjoy a remarkably high level of intellectual accomplishments. Out of the 543 members, 260 either had a post-graduate or higher degree or a technical degree (several of the parliamentarians curiously have a law degree). An additional 157 had under-graduate degrees. Thus, four in five members of the 2009 Lok Sabha had an under-graduate or higher degree. There was also a strong pattern of a larger proportion of candidates winning as we move from less educated to more educated groups of candidates. Not only well educated, but members of the 2009 Lok Sabha were also a wealthy lot. Based on officially acknowledged wealth, one in five members of the 2009 Lok Sabha was a dollar millionaire (₹5 crore or more). Almost another two in five were rupee crorepatis. The silver lining, however, was that those with minimal wealth did participate in elections in large numbers even though their success rate was low. Two out of every five candidates in the 2009 elections had wealth below ₹5 lakh. Of these, 14 won the elections.

The most disconcerting feature of the Parliament, however, was the presence of a large number of members with criminal cases pending against them. The proportion of those with one or more criminal cases registered against them was 14 per cent among candidates but 30 per cent among elected members. Thus, the victory rate was seemingly higher among the accused than among the 'clean' candidates. Indeed, detailed data show a steadily rising

---

[2] The section draws on Gupta and Panagariya (2011a).

trend of victory rate as we move from groups of candidates with no accusations to those with a larger number of cases registered against them. We revert to this issue in the next section.

Based on this information, if one were to construct a winning candidate with average characteristics, he would be a wealthy male (with mean assets worth ₹60 million and median assets worth ₹12 million) in his mid-fifties, with at least an under-graduate degree. He would come from one of the main political parties. There is a 30 per cent chance that he would have at least one criminal case against him and a 15 per cent chance that he would have two or more criminal cases pending against him, a 14 per cent chance that he would have at least one serious criminal case registered against him. There is also a 34 per cent probability that he had served as an MP in the previous Parliament.

Candidate characteristics versus party affiliation

Even as the characteristics of candidates, which could in turn signal their competence, seem important in determining who will be elected to Parliament, these turn out to be far less important in explaining the outcomes than their party affiliations. The fact that hardly any independent candidates or candidates from smaller parties won elections suggests that this is the case. How can one explain the better performance of candidates from larger parties, that is, national or state parties, in elections? It could simply be that the larger parties field candidates with better electoral prospects. The other possible reasons could be that voters are more familiar with candidates from larger parties since they have a longer track record; prefer them because of their ideology or caste identity; or that the larger parties have a stronger network of party workers to help campaign and more resources at their disposal to spend on election campaigns, all of which influence voters in their favour.

In order to consider the first possible explanation we compare the various observable characteristics of candidates from larger parties with those of the other candidates. Table 4.2 shows that candidates fielded by larger parties were somewhat older, more

Table 4.2 Comparing the characteristics of the candidates of larger parties and others (averages)

	Percentage of votes obtained	Age of the candidates (in years)	Wealth (in log)	Percentage of incumbents	Percentage of female candidates	Percentage of candidates with criminal charges
Candidates from large parties	19.9	50.5	15.4	16	8	13
Other candidates	1.20	43.7	13.1	0.3	6.6	4.5

Source: Author's calculations using the data from the Association for Democratic Reforms (ADR) (http://myneta.info).

educated, wealthier, a larger percentage of them were incumbent MPs, and a larger percentage of them were women.[3]

However, a different profile of the candidates is perhaps not the only reason why candidates from larger parties performed significantly better than candidates from smaller parties or independent candidates. It cannot, for example, explain the rather poor performance of Meera Sanyal, a professional banker with ABN Amro Bank, who contested the elections as an independent candidate from the Mumbai South constituency in Maharashtra in 2009. Altogether, 20 candidates contested the elections from Mumbai South, out of which nine contested as independents, with Sanyal being one of them. The remaining 11 candidates had some party affiliation, five were affiliated to a national or a state party, two were affiliated to important regional parties in Maharashtra (Maharashtra Navnirman Sena and the Shiv Sena) and the remaining four were from smaller political parties.

Sanyal's credentials may be considered impeccable: she was one of the most educated candidates in the fray, had no criminal charges against her, was relatively wealthy and well intentioned as well. However, she managed to garner only 10,000 odd votes, that is, 1.5 per cent of the total votes. The winner, Milind Deora

---

[3] Incidentally, a larger proportion of them also face criminal charges.

from the Congress party who possessed impressive credentials of his own, obtained 272,411 votes, that is, about 42 per cent of the total votes.[4] At the second and third place were candidates from the Maharashtra Navnirman Sena and Shiv Sena respectively, who faced one criminal charge each (and were somewhat less wealthy). These candidates also managed to get a large number of votes—25 and 23 per cent of the total votes respectively; and the vote share of the fourth candidate (from the Bahujan Samaj Party) was still respectable at 5 per cent of the total.

The wide divergence in the performance of Sanyal and Deora or that of the other leading candidates cannot be attributed to their different personal attributes and achievements. Our reading is that despite the fact that many of the factors were on her side, there was one crucial factor which went against Sanyal. She lacked affiliation with a political party, that is, either a national or a state or a regional party dominant in the state. One implication that follows is that well-intentioned Indian citizens who want to contribute to nation building and improve the political discourse by joining Parliament need to first win the support and affiliation of a large national or state party in order to win elections.

The importance of existing large parties in electoral success may decline in India if following its success, the newly formed Aam Aadmi Party (AAP), in the 2013 Delhi assembly elections, comes to have a sizeable presence in the rest of India. Many intellectuals, social activists and professions, much like Sanyal, seem to view it as a viable alternative to contesting elections as independent candidates or to staying away from politics altogether. Indeed, Sanyal has already joined AAP and may contest an election in 2014 as its candidate. It will be interesting to see whether a new party such as AAP will be able to reduce the advantage enjoyed by the older parties, and particularly, whether Sanyal will fare better than she did as an independent candidate.

---

[4] The fact that Mr Deora's father had been an incumbent and a union minister in the UPA government possibly helped his electoral performance as well.

Incumbency

In principle, incumbency in India can be defined not only for the sitting members of the Lok Sabha, but also for the party in power at the Centre (candidates of the largest party or all the parties that formed a ruling coalition, as well as for the party in power in each state (candidates of the parties in power in the states at the time of the 2009 general elections).

Gupta and Panagariya (2012) analyse the role of incumbency in election outcomes at all the three levels. The information they collected shows that almost 70 per cent of the outgoing members contested the elections in 2009, and almost half of them won the elections. Thus, more than one-third of the members returned to the Lok Sabha. Looking at the data systematically, the authors find that while there was a definite incumbency advantage at all the three levels, this advantage was mediated by the performance of the ruling party in the state, which we turn to next.

Performance of incumbent parties in states

We measure performance as the average economic growth in the states from the beginning of the fiscal year 2004–05 to the end of 2008–09. This period approximately coincides with the period between the May 2004 and May 2009 general elections and also defines the approximate period of incumbency in the states. We rank the larger states, 19 of them, in a declining order of the average growth rate and divide them into three groups: high, medium and low growth. Figure 4.2 gives the deviation of the average growth in a state's domestic product from the national GDP growth for each of the 19 states with the states stacked in declining order in terms of their growth rates. The dotted lines in turn divide the states into a high-growth group with seven states and low- and medium-growth groups of six states each.

We define the incumbent party as the main ruling party (or two main ruling parties when power is shared) if it was in power at least between 2005 and 2007. If there was an election for the

Figure 4.2   Difference between the average growth rate of state domestic product and the GDP growth rate (2004–08)

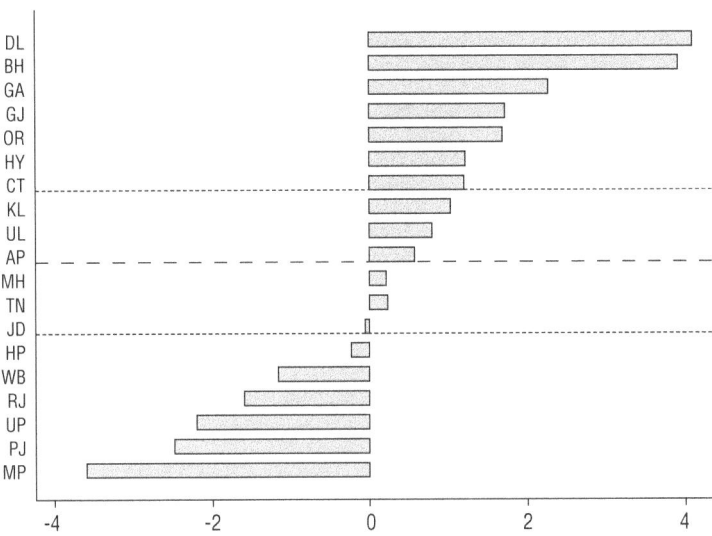

Source: Gupta and Panagariya (2014).

state legislative assembly in 2008 or 2009 and the party ruling until 2007 lost this election, it was still considered the incumbent party for purposes of the national elections held in April–May 2009. The underlying logic is that the electorate would treat the party that was in government for several years prior to 2009 responsible for the policies and performance of the state rather than the party that took over the government in the year just preceding the general elections.

The key question we ask is: what proportion of the candidates fielded by the state incumbent party won the national elections? The outcome is depicted in Figure 4.3. Remarkably, incumbent parties in the high-growth states won 85 per cent of the seats that they contested. In contrast, those in medium- and low-growth states could win only approximately 52 and 40 per cent of the seats contested respectively. This strong relationship between growth performance and election outcomes is obtained through econometric methods by Gupta and Panagariya (2014). Quantitatively, the effect of growth

Figure 4.3 Proportion of the candidates of the incumbent party in the state winning the national election (sorted by the state's growth rates)

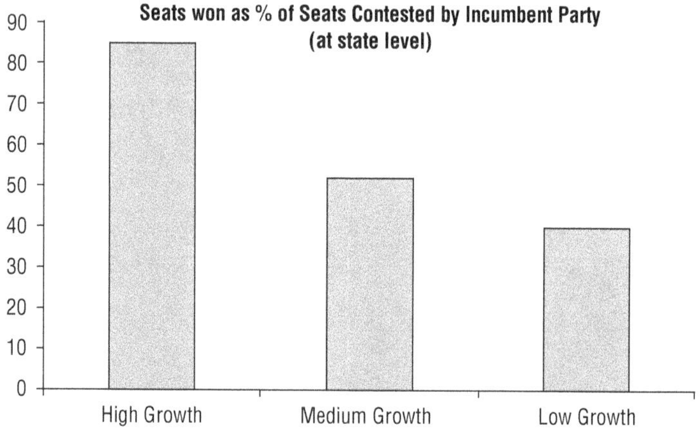

Source: Gupta and Panagariya (2012).

was found to be much larger than the effect of candidates' personal characteristics or their party affiliations.

Explaining the superior performance of the Congress in 2009 elections[5]

As discussed earlier, the 2009 parliamentary elections returned the Congress party to power with more seats than even the most optimistic predictions. From 145 seats in 2004, the Congress increased its tally to 206 seats. Attributing this gain to the stellar growth performance at the national level, as done by some in the Indian press, is too simplistic because the Congress's electoral performance varied widely across states. For instance, it won just nine out of the 72 seats in Bihar, Odisha and Chhattisgarh. Despite the high growth that they experienced, these states voted overwhelmingly against the Congress. Clearly we need a more nuanced analysis to explain the increase in the Congress tally.

Our analysis in the previous section offers a part of the explanation: the Congress was able to retain and perhaps even

---

[5] This section draws on Gupta (2011).

increase its tally in states that it had ruled in and where the growth performance was superior. For example, in Haryana and Delhi, two of the fastest growing states, where the Congress was the incumbent party, it won most of the parliamentary seats, increasing its tally from 15 seats in 2004 to 16 seats in 2009 out of a total of 17 seats. But this factor by itself is not sufficient to explain the increase in Congress' tally from 145 in 2004 to 206 in 2009.

A larger part of the gains made by the Congress comes from states that had non-Congress governments and did not perform well economically. In these states, state-incumbent parties lost a large number of seats, which the Congress and its allies were able to pick up. Table 4.3 provides details of the gains made by the Congress. In Madhya Pradesh, Punjab, Rajasthan and Uttar Pradesh where the Congress was in the opposition and the growth record of the incumbent state governments turned out to be poor, it made huge gains, picking up 42 extra seats. The Congress's ally, the Trinamool Congress, made similar gains in West Bengal, another slow-growing state ruled by a rival party. It added 17 seats to its tally in the state, making it easier for the Congress to put together a coalition government. The Congress more or less maintained its 2004 position in most of the medium-growth states with Kerala as the major exception. In that state, Congress added 13 seats though it also lost three seats between Jharkhand and Uttarakhand.

This analysis still does not tell us why the Congress was a major beneficiary of the losses incurred by incumbent parties in states with non-Congress governments that performed poorly, economically.

Table 4.3 Additions to the Congress tally in 2009 over 2004 election

	High-growth states	Medium-growth states	Low-growth states
Congress government	1 (Delhi, Haryana)	8 (Andhra Pradesh, Maharashtra)	
Non-Congress Government	2 (Bihar, Odisha, Chhattisgarh, Gujarat)	10 (Jharkhand, Kerala, Uttarakhand)	42 (Madhya Pradesh, Punjab, Rajasthan and Uttar Pradesh

Source: Author's own calculations.

While it predicts losses to the incumbent party, it does not explain why the voters then chose candidates of one or the other party. There is some tentative evidence that the main opposition party is a major beneficiary when voters reject incumbents but further work is required to establish this hypothesis more definitively.

While one cannot predict the outcome in future elections accurately on the basis of this analysis, what one can conclude from it is that the outcome may be expected to depend significantly on the growth record of incumbent state governments. Our results also suggest that it will be too naïve to predict election results based solely on the anti-incumbency factor, as done by some pundits in future elections. A more careful approach will combine the status of incumbency of various parties in state governments with their performance as incumbents.

Candidates with criminal charges

Why do the candidates with criminal charges do well in elections?

As we saw in the previous section, there is a sizeable presence of candidates and winning candidates who bear criminal charges in Indian elections. The picture, however, is more nuanced than what is often painted in the media. For a start, it must be understood that under the Constitution, no one sentenced to imprisonment of two or more years for a criminal offence is permitted to contest elections. Therefore, none of the candidates, let alone elected members, can be actual criminals sentenced to two or more years behind bars. The popular perception and assertion that a third of Parliament consists of criminals is, thus, exaggerated.

Second, data on criminal charges is likely to be subject to some errors: there may be candidates who are accused of crimes they have not committed, and there may also be candidates who have not been accused but have committed crimes.

Third, it is important to recognize that not all charges involve serious crimes. For example, under Sections 143 and 149 of the Indian Penal Code (IPC), a person can be sentenced to two or more years in prison for merely participating in an unlawful rally. Likewise, Section 148 of the IPC allows the violation of an order by a public servant to be punished by two or more years in prison. The Association for Democratic Reforms (ADR) rightly classifies these charges as 'non-serious' even though conviction under them would bar an individual from contesting elections.

Evidence from other countries shows that when the information about corrupt politicians is made available to voters, it influences their voting decisions, resulting in corrupt politicians getting fewer votes in their re-election bids. On the contrary, in India though it has been almost a decade since the information on criminal charges against candidates was made public and disseminated widely by civil agencies, it seems the voters have not really factored this in their voting decisions in any significant way. Thus, not only does a large percentage of candidates with criminal charges contest elections, as earlier, but an equally large percentage of them also get elected.

One reason why candidates facing criminal cases fare well in elections could be that voters have a preference for candidates belonging to their own ethnic groups irrespective of candidate characteristics. This implies that a politician belonging to the ethnically dominant group in a constituency may win even if he is of lower *quality* (as suggested by Banerjee and Pande 2007).

Another possibility is that in the constituencies in which they contest, all major candidates have such cases pending against them, thus leaving the voters little choice (the 'there is no alternative' hypothesis). However, in general, in each constituency, voters do have a choice between candidates with serious charges and candidates with no serious charges against them. Of the 231 constituencies in which there were candidates with serious criminal charges against them, in 152 none of the other two candidates from the top three candidates had serious charges against them. In 31 constituencies there were two out of three top candidates, who had charges against them, and only in six constituencies all three of the top three candidates had charges against them. So the view that voters do not have a viable alternative does not seem to hold currency.

Table 4.4 A Comparison of candidates with and without criminal charges[6]

	% Votes	Age	Log assets (in 1,000s)	Education Index	Incumbent (per cent)
Candidates without criminal charges	5.9	45.7	13.7	2.57	4
Candidates with criminal charges	15.4***	47.2***	15.1***	2.71***	10***
Total	6.59	45.8	13.81	2.58	5

Source: Dutta and Gupta (2014).
Note: *** indicates that the values of the respective variables for candidates with charges and other candidates without criminal charges are significantly different from each other at the 1 per cent level of significance.

The most promising explanation for why candidates with criminal charges fare well in elections seems to be that they are wealthy; Dutta and Gupta (2014) find evidence to corroborate this hypothesis (also see Table 4.4). They show that while voters tend to penalize candidates with criminal charges, they also tend to vote for wealthier candidates. This positive effect of wealth on the vote share is higher for the candidates with criminal charges, than for the candidates who do not face such charges. In addition, a large number of these 'tainted' candidates are affiliated to a large party, and some of them may be incumbents, and therefore, enjoy the associated benefits of name recognition, patronage and access to the official machinery.

Criminality and corruption[7]

Our analysis also shows that the presence of a sizeable number of members with pending criminal charges against them in Parliament does not necessarily have to do with the level of corruption in the government. None of the members charged with bribery and corruption in the second UPA government's tenure—A. Raja, Suresh Kalmadi and Kanimozhi—had a single criminal charge against them. Nor did some well-known perpetrators of corruption in the cabinet have criminal charges pending against them. Thus, in

[6] Candidates with charges are the candidates who faced at least two charges.
[7] Discussion draws on Gupta and Panagariya (2011b).

thinking about how to reform the system, it is important to treat corruption and the presence of potential criminals in Parliament as separate issues. Regarding the latter, as a minimalist measure the media and NGOs should exert pressure on the governments against appointing members facing serious criminal charges to positions of power. Naming and shaming ministers with serious criminal charges may discourage their appointment.

In terms of serious reforms, a reform suggested by Bimal Jalan, a former member of the Rajya Sabha, seems the most promising. Accordingly, cases against those elected to legislative bodies should be subjected to time-bound disposal. In this manner, one can preserve individuals' right to contest elections without being proven guilty. At the same time, it will ensure that those who know that the cases against them are tight and will result in conviction will refrain from entering the fray to avoid speedy trials.

However, what makes the reform of the system politically difficult is that among the contestants, those with criminal charges or even serious charges are spread across all major political parties. As Table 4.5 shows state parties have the largest proportion of candidates who face at least two criminal charges, followed by national parties, which fielded more than a tenth of the candidate facing such charges. Smaller parties and independents had a smaller proportion among them who faced such charges.

Looking at some of the largest parties, in the 2009 elections of a total of 440 candidates that the Congress fielded, 52 had serious criminal charges pending against them. The numbers were

Table 4.5 Candidates with criminal cases across party types

Party Type	Number of candidates	Number of candidates with least 2 criminal cases	% of candidates with at least 2 criminal cases
	I	II	$III: (II/I)*100$
National parties	1,353	176	11.5
State parties	585	108	15.6
Unrecognized parties	1,790	110	6.2
Independent candidates	3,659	124	3.4

Source: Dutta and Gupta (2014).

not too dissimilar for the BJP: 48 candidates with serious criminal charges out of a total of 431. Proportionately, Lalu Yadav's Rashtriya Janata Dal (RJD) took the cake, fielding 11 out of 44, or a hefty 25 per cent of the candidates, with serious criminal charges. All India Anna Dravida Munnetra Kazhagan (AIADMK) from Tamil Nadu came a close second with five out of 23 facing serious charges. Remarkably, only one out of 22 contestants put up by Dravida Munnetra Kazhagan (DMK), whose candidates have figured prominently in the 2G scandal, had serious criminal charges pending against them.

Conclusion

Using the data for the 2009 parliamentary elections, we discussed the factors that influence election outcomes. We found that even though individual characteristics matter, and party affiliations matter as well, one important factor which dwarfs the effect of all other factors, is economic performance under incumbent state governments. Voters forcefully vote in favour of parties which deliver high growth and reject the ones which do not. Incumbents who deliver high growth in states are rewarded in elections at the Centre as well. We also touched upon the reasons candidates with criminal charges fare well in elections, and pointed to the 'wealth advantage' that they enjoy. Our view is that reducing their presence will require a consensus among parties—since they are widespread across all parties—eliminating their wealth advantage and making the convictions against them speedier.

While one cannot predict outcomes in future elections in India based on the discussion in this essay, what one can conclude is that the outcome will significantly depend on the growth record of state economies under incumbent state governments. Our results also suggest that in future elections it will be naïve to predict results based solely on the anti-incumbency factor, as has been done by some scholars in the past. A careful approach will combine the incumbency status of various parties in the states, with the economic performance of these states during their tenure in power.

While a common theme across the essays in this book is that political considerations affect the choices that the policymakers make, the main message that comes out of our research, summarized in this essay, is that the voters have increasingly been rewarding good performance or good policy choices. This is reflected not just in the results of the elections at the central level, but perhaps is also seen in elections to assemblies in several states such as Bihar, Odisha and Delhi, where performing governments, across parties were re-elected for several subsequent terms. These observations only affirm that the electorate is intelligent and while politicians may try a 'politics first agenda', voters regard performance as important and the wiser of the politicians should take note of this.

References

Banerjee, Abhijit V. and Rohini Pande. (2007). 'Parochial Politics: Ethnic Preferences and Political Corruption', CEPR Discussion Papers 6381.

Dutta, Bhaskar and Poonam Gupta. (2014). 'Why are the Candidates with Criminal Charges Elected in India?', *Economic and Political Weekly*, XLIX (4).

Gupta, Poonam. (2011). 'For Performers, Incumbency Helps', The *Financial Express*, 19 April. Available at: http://www.financialexpress.com/news/column-for-performers-incumbency-helps/777847.

Gupta, Poonam and Arvind Panagariya. (2011a). 'Our Parliamentarians: Rich, Educated, Criminal?': The *Times of India*. Available at: http://articles.timesofindia.indiatimes.com/2011-04-05/edit-page/29380605_1_candidates-formal-education-educational-qualifications.

———. (2011b). 'Crime tainted MPs have little to do with high-level corruption', The *Economic Times*. Available at: http://articles.economictimes.indiatimes.com/2011-09-21/news/30184646_1_criminal-charges-criminal-offence-corruption.

———. (2012). 'India: Election outcomes and economic reforms', in J. Bhagwati and A. Panagariya (eds), *India's Reforms: How they Produced Inclusive Growth*. New York: Oxford University Press, pp. 51–87.

———. (2014). 'Growth and Election Outcomes in a Developing Country', Economics and Politics (forthcoming).

GOVERNANCE

Chapter 5

Institutions, Incentives and Interests in Indian Democracy[1]

Ashima Goyal

Introduction

Inclusive democratic institutions increase the chance of making policy choices that create broad-based prosperity. So it is puzzling that India, which started out with universal suffrage at independence, has made slow progress. Although it adopted a democracy with highly inclusive political institutions, extractive economic institutions inherited from the British, were strengthened as economic controls gave officials more discretionary powers. In addition, a heterogeneous electorate allowed politicians to cultivate vote banks and populist schemes instead of delivering better governance. So a combination of ideas and of structure has made economic institutions dysfunctional. Institutions are

[1] This is a revised and abridged version of a paper presented at the 2012 CDS-NMML conference on 'The Indian Economy: A Longer and Broader View' in New Delhi. I thank Pulapre Balakrishnan for the invitation and useful comments, discussant E. Sridharan and other participants for valuable discussions.

congealed structures and ideas.[2] They give rise to incentives and interests that create persistence. Interests could hijack democratic institutions that ideas and structures have weakened.

But a change in ideas and an increase in the proportion that benefits from growth are strengthening institutions. There is a steady deepening of horizontal democracy or social networks contrasted with the vertical state hierarchy. India's opening out was flexible but was sometimes used as a substitute for harder domestic reforms. It, however, added to the growing constituencies that benefit from growth, and so push for more inclusive economic institutions that enable productivity, not just redistribution. Multiple and diverse interest groups create better institutions and incentives.

Critical changes in governance are slow. Even so, they are happening and are illustrated through aspects of governance and in Centre–state relations. This messy and prolonged process made growth volatile, but to the extent that appropriate institutional change is occurring, growth could be more sustainable.

Ideas

Despite being a closed economy for much of the post-independence period, India has always been open to ideas. The government-led big push and control of economic heights were frontier international development ideas at the time of independence. But, as the many failures of a government-led approach in the socialist bloc and in other stagnating economies became obvious, the weight of Indian policy opinion began to favour markets. The committee mode of functioning, however, made change slow. Moreover, repeated global financial crises made the flaws of markets obvious so the reforms adopted were nuanced despite the current Indian policy

---

[2] The SIIO paradigm (Goyal 2013: 1), which examines how 'structure and ideas become engraved in institutions that affect outcomes', is a useful way to analyze the interaction. The domestic structure relevant to the analysis in this paper is a heterogeneous electorate. SIIO stands for structure, ideas, institutions and outcomes.

elite being largely those with a tendency to rely too much on free markets. A richer domestic debate combined with current frontier thinking can give India a chance to design policies that bring out the best of both governments and markets while suiting conditions on the ground.

For such a process, it is necessary to move away both from an extreme rightist viewpoint for which all problems are due to not opening out and liberalizing enough, and from an extreme leftist viewpoint from which the opening out and the growing role of the private sector have increased inequality and stressed the social fabric. Liberalization was easier to do than improving domestic governance but foreign capital will not continue to finance current account deficits in an economy where appropriate domestic infrastructure is not created. Neither the government nor the people can directly run the economy, so firms and markets must play a role, but with competition and appropriate regulation.

Although India persisted in an increasingly inappropriate path for a long time, certain strengths were built up. For example, its skilled English-educated labour allowed it to catch the outsourcing wave. The planning process did create a diverse economy—a major current strength that was enhanced by reforms.

The Spence Commission (2008) examined 13 economies that in the period after 1950, grew at above 7 per cent for more than 25 years. Nine of these were in Asia. Their common characteristics included openness, macroeconomic stability, high savings and investment rates and market allocation of resources. Governments were capable—pragmatic and flexible rather than ideological. While willing to intervene in markets to promote exports through industrial policies and to manage exchange rates (with the use of some capital controls and reserve accumulation), they were flexible enough not to get locked into distorting policies and to anticipate and change policies as required for growth. Resource mobility and urbanization were supported. Public investment in infrastructure accounted for 5 to 7 per cent of GDP or more. Specific contextual interventions and the microeconomic incentives that were created were important. External drivers and opening out alone did not create growth.

India and China, the countries currently catching up, also followed policies far from standard reform prescriptions. But compared to China's performance, India's catch-up growth has been volatile. Although China is a one-party dictatorship, it shows a more pragmatic response to emerging bottlenecks given its strategy of 'crossing the river while feeling the stones'. In democratic India, prevailing ideas and ideology are more difficult to change.

Political constraints on policymaking explain the Indian government's neglect of investment and governance in the post-reforms period. Inadequate policies are followed not out of ignorance, but because of deeper political considerations. Democracy must deepen before it can deliver. How did this happen in western democracies?

Inclusive democratic institutions

Acemoglu and Robinson (AR) (2012) argue that a state must be strong to be effective, but strength can imply a coercive pursuit of individual rather than of national interest. For a state to create broad-based wealth, inclusive democratic institutions must temper its power.[3] Such institutions increase the probability of success for a nation since they generate the creative destruction and innovation that sustain wealth.

British and French history illustrates the process. Both Britain and France established Parliaments and followed the rule of law. The power sharing this entailed weakened the absolute power of monarchs. The overthrow of King James II of England, and the French Revolution, succeeded because broad and diverse political groupings had emerged such as commercial and upwardly mobile farmers, different kinds of manufacturers, and Atlantic traders, who

---

[3] Although strong political centralization allowed the Soviet or Chinese state to coordinate resource allocation and grow, the authors expect such growth to be limited as a dominant state blocks innovation for fear of loss of power. Even if newcomers take power, they face few constraints and seek to maintain gains from allowing extractive institutions to persist.

could benefit from creative destruction. As Parliament empowered a broad and strong coalition against Stuart absolutism, especially by the standards of the time, England became a constitutional monarchy.

In much of history, elites routinely enjoyed special privileges. The rule of law replaces such privileges with rights that apply equally to all. Broad segments of society are willing to push back attempts to vitiate the rule of law because under more inclusion the potential benefits of monopoly power are no longer worth the risks. This restrains absolute power and creates more inclusive institutions and policy. Power sharing under pluralistic political institutions prevents any one element from trying to get more power.

Economic inclusion

More inclusive political institutions made economic institutions more inclusive and eventually led to the Industrial Revolution. Domestic monopolies were abolished in 1640. After 1688, the Parliament strengthened property rights eroded under the Stuarts. It prevented arbitrary taking away of rights. Obscure property rights were simplified and made secure. Since rights to revenue could no longer be abrogated, private participation in infrastructure building was encouraged.

The Parliament began to promote manufacturing, rather than taxing and restricting it. The hated 'hearth tax' (AR: 194) which fell largely on industry, was abolished in 1689. New parliamentarians from Manchester and Birmingham wanted cheap food and low wages, so the Corn Laws which banned grain import, keeping prices high and benefiting large landowners, were repealed in 1846. The Parliament could be petitioned and was likely to implement petitions that collected many signatures. Policy now favoured the many not the few. For example, it was more likely to help industry broadly rather than just a few industrialists.

The education system was made more accessible to the masses. The Education Act of 1870 made the government responsible for the systematic provision of universal education, which was made free of charge in 1891. The school-leaving age was raised and special provisions were made for children from poor families. The Liberal Party, in the early years of the twentieth century, began providing public services such as health and unemployment insurance, government-financed pensions and minimum wages. As a result, taxes rose many times and fell more on the wealthy.

Thus, the characteristics of inclusive economic institutions are competitive entry, low broad-based taxes, absence of arbitrariness in policy and public services that enhance human capital equitably. Why has India, which started with full political inclusion, not been able to achieve economic inclusion?

India: Political but not economic inclusion

Unlike Britain where universal suffrage took a long time in coming, India started with it. The west was very sceptical about the survival of Indian democracy, partly because of the 'unwashed hordes' invading the hallowed precincts of Parliament (Guha 2007). Their own history was one of a very slow and careful extension of suffrage.

AR regard India's failures as due to the extractive institutions that the British left it with, despite the British-style democratic institutions that were set-up at independence. In AR's geography-based argument, colonial powers established extractive institutions when they did not intend to settle in a country, perhaps because of the climate. But the British did stay in India for hundreds of years and built courts, railways and universities.

A country of large size and heterogeneous provinces needed strong central control. It may have been to achieve this that the British established a unique centralized administrative service. This, however, had an ethos of superiority and the distance of ruling elites, which it retains. The federal structure also led to multiple levels of government and agencies. All these aspects lowered accountability to the local populace. Despite political inclusion, the prevailing philosophy of economic controls gave the new indigenous government large discretionary powers. So they could further increase the extractive powers of the institutions that they had inherited at independence.

In addition, the possibility of creating vote blocks in a heterogeneous electorate, led to vote buying and populist policies that targeted specific groups. The caste system, whose origin and rationale were economic, was widely expected to die out with modern economic development. Gupta (2000) shows how through history the caste system had evolved in response to economic pressures. It was economic stagnation that tended to proliferate and strengthen caste hierarchies.[4] Since there was stagnation post-independence in the closed and controlled economy, castes were strengthened and organized to fight for rights. Caste-based policies to create vote banks sustained the caste system. Thus, caste allowed politicians to get away with stagnation, and stagnation further strengthened caste. But it was now a political identity, not a system of economic organization.

There is an argument that it was caste interests that weakened strong legal institutions that the British left behind. Loopholes left for caste subverted laws. However, the causality may be the opposite, running from institutions to caste. Ideas of government control strengthened extractive institutions, resulting in stagnation. In these circumstances, it was politically expedient to use structural heterogeneity to create caste-based vote banks. This created and strengthened interest groups which allowed the political class to bypass delivery of public services despite inclusive political institutions.

So the process of universal suffrage leading to inclusive economic institutions, that raise productivity, remains inadequate

---

[4] There are signs of higher post-reforms growth in reducing caste distinctions. Kapur et al. (2010) found that lower castes were now eating ritual upper caste foods in festivals in the villages they studied. Prasad and Kumble (2012) report on research that finds that dalits succeed most in new and caste-neutral occupations; reform opportunities suit dalit enterpreneurs. They found that Delhi's Azadpur fruit and vegetable mandi did not have a single dalit *adhatiya* or middleman, since traditional castes dominate these established occupations.

in India. But caste-based and other interest groups were not the primary cause of stagnation.

Governance: Institutional hysteresis

Indian government administration performs very poorly. Cumbersome procedures hinder infrastructure investment, although it is greatly required since inadequate infrastructure makes daily living hazardous. The death of Mahi, a five-year-old girl in 2012, after she fell into a drain because a manhole cover was missing, created countrywide outrage. The criminal justice system is in shambles—with the number of policemen and judges ratio to population much below world averages. J. Sinha, of the Boston Consulting Group, got a large response from readers when he wrote about the travails of providing an acceptable identity proof to a bank, given poorly thought through regulatory requirements (the *Economic Times* 11 July 2012). Regulation of drugs in India comes under four government departments leading to delays in permissions that can range from six months to two years, compared to the practice in some countries that if permission does not come in 28 days, it is regarded as given. There are also conflicts of interest. Since the pharmaceutical industry comes under the chemical ministry, the latter bats for the industry (the *Economic Times* 10 July 2012).

There is no shortage of potential improvements. Stroke-of-the-pen reforms are possible. Successive expenditure reform commissions made useful suggestions for re-organizing administration, reducing multiple clearances, departmental overlaps and establishing clear accountability. The cabinet accepted these but did not implement them. Problems with infrastructure clearances clearly highlight the bottlenecks that the current administrative structure creates. Systemic problems create de-motivated and fearful bureaucrats—but the latter are not the source of the problem as is commonly believed.

Many laws, unchanged since colonial times, give too much power to the administration. Some of the laws are so unreasonable that no one can follow them. Since everyone can be found guilty, they give a tool to a corrupt or unreasonable official to extort or victimize, using the laws. But ill-defined laws can also be used to victimize the administrators themselves. For example, a clause in the Prevention of Corruption Act (1988) defines criminal misconduct by a public servant to include obtaining a 'pecuniary advantage' without some 'public interest' involved. Ensuring this is difficult in a market economy. Ill-designed APMC acts allow insiders to capture mandis, choking agricultural retail resulting in steep food inflation. All these laws need to be re-drafted. Clearer responsibilities can enhance outcomes and reputations of public servants.

An ex-IAS officer responding to Mahi's death blamed the absence of accountability. The superior tells the inferior to do something, he tells the line department, but there is no follow up. In his view, an individual officer can still achieve much if he were to use his many powers. As a district magistrate, he got work done by a contractor when the line department did not do it, and deducted the money from the engineer's payment. The latter appealed to the courts but the deduction was upheld (the *Times of India* 30 June 2012). Very few individuals are willing to fight a system, however. This has to change and institutional hysteresis has to be overcome.

In China, the government coordinates well since officials are accountable to the party boss. In India elections make voters' priorities crucial. But if voters can be split into clearly identified vote banks, and government schemes and power used for patronage, performance is not crucial for re-election. So only a change in voters' priorities can trigger change. Systemic political reforms are also required such as in political funding and in changing the first-past-the-post electoral system that delivers unstable coalitions. Jalan (2013) suggests extending the anti-defection bill from individuals to parties. So if a small coalition partner leaves a government in mid-stream its seats would be up for re-election—reducing its ability to extract concessions and hold-up law-making and reducing the incentive to form new parties.

A key systemic change is improving the coordination between the Centre and the states. The most critical Indian policy initiatives are in areas such as agriculture, health, education, policing and making India one market that are all on the concurrent list of the Constitution. Excessive centralization under the British[5] was initially strengthened due to concerns for national integration. The Constitution mandated an inter-state council but a strong central government in the early years and the emphasis on planning, denied it the weight required. As the political system fragmented and regional parties came up, the states obtained more political freedom but coordination between the Centre and the states became very poor. Market-facilitating tax harmonization is held up for lack of support by some big consumer states who fear they will lose revenue.

The Constitution clearly demarcates taxation powers between the Centre and the states in India's fiscal union and lays down revenue sharing criteria, which periodic finance commissions revisit. Equity criteria that mandate higher awards to weaker states are an essential part of making it one country. Rath (2012) argues the focus on planning made the government persuade a constitutional body, charged with making grants-in-aid to bring states to a uniform level of public services, to cede grant-making powers to the Planning Commission. But the latter made transfers according to the Plans to build industry and not to provide public services to the people. Additional transfers possible under Article 282 of the Constitution became dominant, accounting for as much as one-third of state spending. Multiple centrally sponsored schemes, administered through the Planning Commission, undermined the authority of the finance commissions. The Gadgil formula applies to only a fraction of the transfers so they are increasingly discretionary.

Tight restrictions on end use and delays in sanctions reduce the utility of the transfers for state governments. But the latter

---

[5] The centralized federalism of the British 1935 Government of India Act was largely adopted in the Constitution (Granville, 2002, p. 158).

are guilty of the same treatment of lower-level bodies such as municipalities and panchayats, which are denied financial and functional independence. Decentralization needed to be strengthened in the Constitution and this was attempted with the 73rd and 74th amendments on direct local-level democracy in the 1990s but implementation remains uneven with some states able to use 'may' clauses to resist effective devolution. But decentralization is also not a panacea. It could strengthen local elites who repress those lower down in the social hierarchy. Apart from strengthening community participation and awareness, focusing on the district is a via media.

A critical juncture in India?

Even so, history is not destiny. Although institutions persist, rapid change is possible at critical junctures that disrupts the existing economic or political balance. The change can be in the direction of more extraction or more inclusion. Inclusive ground conditions raise the probability that the path taken will be in the right direction.

In 2013, India met many of the ground conditions for institutional change that AR identify. These include pluralism of interests, a vibrant business class and gradual reforms. The markets that can induce a virtuous cycle of more efficient allocation of resources, acquisition of education and skills and technological innovations, are all there. The country has long had the rule of law and private property even though implementation is poor. Reforms added export demand to strong domestic demand, as manufacturing became globally competitive. The changes added up to a critical mass. Networks of markets and associations became dense, reducing transaction costs as learning occurred and quality improved. It was no longer only the government undertaking initiatives for society. NGOs and corporates[6] became active as well. Other positive factors include the demographic profile and investment in infrastructure that has reached 7 per cent of GDP.

---

[6] See Bhattacharya (2012) for dynamic CSR and business-model based private initiatives that are improving the delivery of essential services such as water and health, which the government has failed to provide.

But as the executive failed to deliver good governance, India saw increasing court activism. For example, Supreme Court orders sought to improve air quality in New Delhi and to investigate corruption in the allocation of natural resources. Legal changes also furthered more inclusion. NGOs and the middle class acquired clout through the mechanism of public interest litigation (PILs) and the Right to Information (RTI) Act. The Right to Education Act was part of a more rights-based activism. Fiscal Responsibility and Budget Management (FRBM) legislation restrained the government's ability to spend.

Popular protests against corruption sought to reduce the government's discretion over resources—a major source of kickbacks. Independent constitutional bodies such as the Election Commission, the Finance Commission and the Comptroller and Auditor General (CAG), became more active in preventing misuse of political power. A fledgling party was able to defeat the powerful incumbent in a crucial 2013 Delhi election on an anti-corruption platform. This deepening horizontal democracy is pushing for better governance.[7] The coalition that gained from government-led redistribution dominated for a long time because of heterogeneity and poverty. But demands for better public services in health, education and infrastructure are increasing as prosperity increases the numbers who stand to benefit from them. Media and low cost telecom raise awareness, making the 'virtual middle class' larger then the actual. Governments act when their own interests are involved.[8] As a result, economic institutions are also slowly becoming more inclusive.

The reforms made government more business-friendly although a balance between extraction of revenue and encouraging business

---

[7] Organizations like the Association for Democratic Reform and Praja are getting politicians to disclose their assets and police records and making report cards on the elected representatives' performance.

[8] Bussell (2012) showed that the states that have less corruption and can reach targeted vote banks (for example, the rural poor), were the ones that implemented e-governance initiatives. Loss of political funding from more transparent e-governance can be a major impediment to change.

growth is yet to be found. Opening out perhaps occurred as the forces that gained from growth strengthened and the reforms strengthened them further. So 'active inclusion', defined as inclusion which creates conditions for the many to contribute to and participate in growth (Goyal 2012), is becoming more acceptable politically. Government intervention remains essential, since externalities limit private investment below optimal levels. But intervention should lead to provision of better public services, thus increasing rewards to work. This is uniquely suited to the Indian catch-up growth and increasingly youthful demographic profile. With these essential background changes, more competition and better incentive structures can improve even general governance and Centre–state relations, where change has been slow. Some examples are now given.

Recent finance commissions have given states incentives to improve their finances and special grants conditional on better types of expenditure, in addition to traditional equity-based transfers. States that signed the FRBM legislation were given special debt forgiveness. These initiatives, together with buoyancy in shared central revenues, led to remarkable improvement in state finances. A viable fiscal union needs transfers plus some discipline. Experience with urban renewal missions, which made part of large central ministry transfers conditional upon improved public services, shows that incentives from non-discretionary mechanisms work best when they are immune to political negotiation.

Even as market borrowings substitute loans from the centre and impose market discipline, while transfers themselves are made more time-bound and outcome-based dialogue should complement incentives. Regular meetings of an invigorated inter-state council could evolve new policy initiatives, not just communicate policy decisions, thus involving states in the initial stages.

The Cabinet Committee on Economic Affairs' (CCEA) 2012 decision to restructure the debt of state electricity distribution utilities (discoms) has some of the required combinations of discipline and support. Therefore, it is likely to work better than a package given 10 years ago that did not prevent the discoms piling up debt again.

The decision to take over 50 per cent of discoms' short-term debt in the next two to five years while providing grants for improvements over and above targets is similar to the debt consolidation and relief facility that the XIIth Finance Commission had given. Grants for improvement will encourage reform measures, while short-term debt restructuring improves discipline.

States are to notify the tariff order for a financial year by end-April, make upfront subsidy payments, meter and monitor the turnaround plan, convert state government loans into equity, involve the private sector and ensure punctual auditing of accounts. The carrot comes from a central government grant equal to the value of additional power saved by reducing technical and commercial losses above a proposed limit. There will also be capital reimbursement support for 25 per cent of the principal repayment by the state government on the liability undertaken under the new proposal.

If the Centre's initiatives improve governance, its own transfers are better designed, delivered and targeted; an increasingly aware electorate will reward it just as it is rewarding better governance in states by re-election. Yardstick competition and convergence will take place across administrations. Witsoe's (2012) study of Bihar shows how large numbers of agents involved in corrupt activities quickly turned to more constructive activities with a regime change.

As some states allow FDI in retail, change labour laws and reform power distribution and do better, others will follow. This happened with the adoption of VAT. As states that implemented it gained revenue, others followed. No one wants to be the last man standing. FDI is slow to come in despite permissions, since other legal and institutional impediments have to be removed first. But over time, it can boost forces making for change.

Figure 5.1 summarizes this argument. It shows how one set of ideas and congealed institutions create perverse incentives and interests. But they can change under a fresh set of ideas and more openness, creating more inclusive economic institutions and deeper horizontal political institutions.

Figure 5.1 From political to economic inclusion

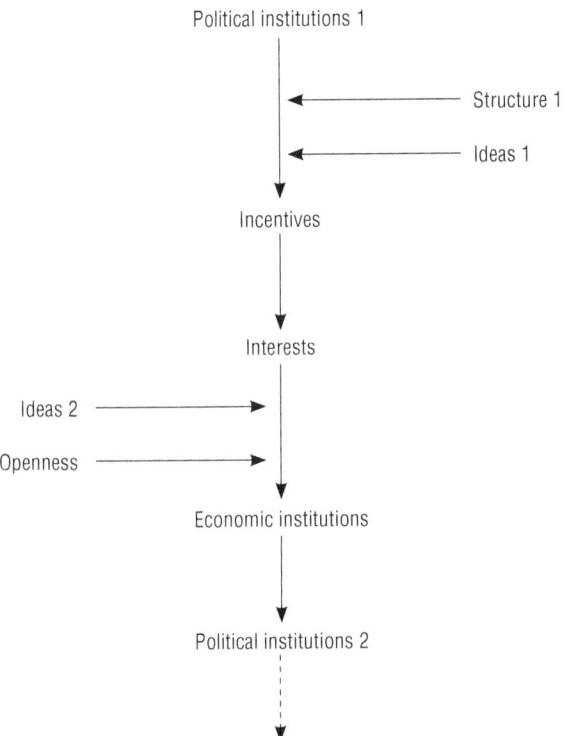

Policymakers at the Centre focused on more opening up because this was something they could do without persuading the states to come along. It was required because India was too closed an economy, but in 2011 and 2012 financing a widening current account deficit proved difficult as foreign inflows fluctuated because of both domestic policy bottlenecks and external risks. So, the difficult task of improving the domestic supply-side must receive priority. This may become feasible as institutions change and provision of better public goods becomes an election issue.

Table 5.1 shows that India lags behind other countries more in health, infrastructure and institutions compared to financial market and business development. So it is clear where more attention is required. Else lagging sectors can choke others.

Table 5.1 India's world position on different criteria

Relative lags in:	India's rank (highest is 1)
Institutions	70
Infrastructure	84
Health and primary education	101
Higher education and training	86
Financial market development	21
Business sophistication	40

Source: The Global Competitiveness Report 2012–2013. World Economic Forum. Available at: http://www3.weforum.org/docs/WEF_GlobalCompetitivenessReport_2012–13.pdf.

Conclusion

After opening out and crossing a threshold, a nation's potential growth is high during the process of catch-up with the frontier. But if domestic distortions force inappropriate polices, growth can slow down due to an inadequate response to internal and external shocks and failure to address emerging bottlenecks. Since political power and interests, as enshrined in institutions, drive policy choices, inclusive political and economic institutions make it more likely that the correct choices that empower broad sections of the population to contribute to and participate in growth are made. Then nations will be more likely to sustain high growth, with enough flexibility to anticipate and adjust policies as required for growth.

India started out with highly inclusive political institutions since it adopted universal suffrage at independence. But extractive economic institutions, inherited from the British, were made more so by the dominant development ideas of the time which favoured economic controls. The heterogeneous electorate, which could be divided by caste, class, community and region, and economic stagnation in the closed government-led economy, allowed politicians to seek re-elections through cultivated vote banks and populist schemes instead of delivering better governance. This is changing.

Change is happening, but if civil society understood it they would push for provision of better schools, roads and hospitals to service disadvantaged groups. Caste-based policies need to give way to better general public services in a new India. Reservations are an example of the old policy set. Special categories constitute more than half of the population. Such widespread reservations will harm productivity. The solution of improving skills becomes easier in a higher-growth economy since many types of occupations requiring varying levels of skills appear. The argument that reservations have not yet created equity, so reservations are required in all types and hierarchies of activities is flawed. Reservations were originally introduced for 10 years. They have lasted for 60 years but have still not delivered. Skill-based access to jobs may do better in the new conditions. That school enrolments rose to 100 per cent, with better opportunities, suggests that people respond more to opportunities.

As the world left India behind, and the dominant development ideas changed to favour more openness, India also adopted liberalizing reforms. Opening out was gradual and nuanced, and this was beneficial since it helped mitigate the impact of the many external crises in this period. But even so, external liberalization was easier to do than many required internal changes, since the latter affected more domestic interest groups. But the temptation to use more opening out and inflows as a substitute for harder domestic reforms is a short-run policy that can dangerously increase dependency in the long-run. Since the only way to attract inflows to finance the current account deficit is to remove supply-side bottlenecks, the government is being pushed to tackle these issues. A change in ideas and a rise in the proportion that benefits from growth are adding to these pressures.

Poor institutions generated interests that favoured stagnancy. But systems and incentives are improving. Examples from general governance show that although the process is messy and prolonged, it is in the right direction. Although catch-up growth has been volatile, India may be able to avoid the middle-income trap if broader sections are systematically empowered for active inclusion. Then it may even do better than China in the long haul.

References

Acemoglu, D. and J.A. Robinson. (2012). *Why Nations Fail: The Origins of Power, Prosperity and Poverty.* New York: Crown.

Bhattacharya, A. (2012). 'Quiet Revolutions'. *Business Today*, 19 August. Available at: http://businesstoday.intoday.in/story/innovation-for-masses/1/186620.html.

Bussell, J. (2012). 'E-Governance and Corruption in the States: Can Technology Serve the Aam Admi?' *Economic and Political Weekly,* 47 (23): 77–85.

Goyal, A. (2012). 'An Appraisal of Five Year Plans and the Future', in *Yojana*, special issue on *An Approach to 12th Five Year Plan–Issues and Challenges,* January.

———. (2013). 'Sustaining Growth: Interests versus Institutions', IGIDR working paper WP-2013-001. Available at: http://www.igidr.ac.in/pdf/publication/WP-2013-001.pdf.

Granville, A. (2002). 'The Expected and the Unintended in Working a Democratic Constitution', in Z. Hasan, E. Shridharan and R. Sudarshan (eds), *India's Living Constitution.* New Delhi: Permanent Black, p. 158.

Guha, R. (2007). *India after Gandhi: The History of the World's Largest Democracy.* London: Macmillan.

Gupta, D. (2000). *Interrogating Caste: Understanding Hierarchy and Difference in Indian Society.* New Delhi: Penguin Books.

Jalan, B. (2013). *Emerging India: Economics, Politics and Reforms.* New Delhi: Penguin Books.

Kapur, D., C.B. Prasad, L. Pritchett and D.S. Babu. (2010). 'Rethinking Inequality: Dalits in Uttar Pradesh in the Market Reform Era', *Economic and Political Weekly*, 45 (35): 39–49. Available at: http://casi.ssc.upenn.edu/system/files/Rethinking+Inequality+DK,+CBP,+LP,+DSB_0.pdf.

Prasad, C.B. and M. Kamble. (2012). 'To Empower Dalits do Away with India's Antiquated Retail Trading System', The *Times of India*, Mumbai Edition, 5 December. Available at: http://articles.timesofindia.indiatimes.com/2012-12-05/edit-page/35595228_1_dicci-dalit-entrepreneurs-kirana-stores.

Rath, N. (2012). 'Economic Origin of Regional and Caste Parties', *Economic and Political Weekly*, 47 (30): 24–28, 28 July.

Spence Commission on Growth and Development. (2008). *The Growth Report: Strategies for Sustained Growth and Inclusive*

Development. Chair M. Spence. Available at: http://go.worldbank. org/FC797ZNZP0.

Witsoe, J. (2012). 'Everyday Corruption and the Political Mediation of the Indian State: An Ethnographic Exploration of Brokers in Bihar', *Economic and Political Weekly*, 47 (6): 47–54, 11 February.

Chapter 6

Corruption, Politics and Governance

Samuel Paul

There is no country in the world in which everything can be provided for by laws, or in which political institutions can prove a substitute for common sense and public morality...
Alexis De Tocqueville

Corruption in public life is a widely debated issue in India. The severity of the problem is reflected in the frequent media exposure of large-scale scams involving governments and the growing anti-corruption protests across the country by ordinary people in recent years. Many observers believe that corruption in public life adversely impacts socioeconomic development, governance and the quality of life of ordinary citizens. There is a growing realization that the role of 'dark money' and muscle power in politics, the consequent policy capture by powerful vested interests and the widespread lack of accountability in the delivery of public services are manifestations of the cancerous spread of corruption that need to be brought under control. Many believe that the spread of corruption is leading to economic and social development being increasingly lopsided and inequitable.

Corruption is believed to be prevalent in the private sector too. Transactions such as procurement, sales and contracts of all kinds, especially those that involve governments, are prone to corruption. Opaque and collusive deals involving boards and owners for personal gain may entail corrupt and unethical practices. Abuses such as insider trading in financial markets also amount to corruption. However, here we focus on corruption in public life as the theme of this volume is 'politics trumps economics'. Once corruption becomes pervasive in the political system, it will invariably lead to policy capture by vested interests with money power, neglect of the rule of law and failure to deliver public services with fairness and efficiency.

Corrupt practices involve both bribe takers and bribe givers. The conventional definition of corruption as 'abuse of public power for private gain,' however, tends to focus solely on the bribe taker.[1] The UK Bribery Act of 2010 takes into account both givers and takers in its definition of corruption:

> Crime of bribery occurs when a person offers, gives or promises to give a 'financial or other advantage' to another individual in exchange for 'improperly performing' such a function or activity. Also covered is the 'offence of being bribed, defined as requesting, accepting, or agreeing to accept such an advantage, in exchange for improperly performing such a function or activity (HM Government 2010).

Over the years, several perspectives have influenced the thinking of the scholars and leaders who have thought about and championed the need to combat corruption. Perhaps the oldest among them is the moral perspective that stems from the belief that corruption is a violation of universal moral values and standards. In this view, such violations are indefensible, and there is no room

---

[1] Robert Klitgaard refers to corruption as $C = M + D - A$, where C = corruption, M = monopoly, D = discretion and A = accountability (see Klitgaard 1988).

for compromise. Corruption cannot be justified on grounds of expediency, material gains, survival or for the protection of the weak. Second, there is an efficiency perspective that justifies the eradication of corruption on the grounds that it harms economic growth and the well-being of countries and peoples (OECD 1997; Collier 2007). This perspective takes a functional view of corruption, focusing on its adverse impacts on the potential economic well-being of society. Corruption in public life, according to this view, tends to reduce investments that are potentially available to countries. It hurts people's productivity. A number of studies, too, have demonstrated the negative impact of corruption on foreign investments. Third, there is the human rights perspective on corruption that views the problem as a violation and denial of basic human rights of citizens.[2] It rejects the notion that tackling corruption through the criminal justice system is the sole answer. Instead, it gives priority to empowering people through recognizing their civil, political, economic, social and cultural rights.

The many faces of corruption

In popular discourse, corruption is viewed as a phenomenon that covers a multitude of sins. In order to understand and tackle it effectively, it is necessary to disaggregate and divide corruption into useful categories. We propose three criteria here for this purpose. The nature and consequences of corruption may vary by the domain, scale and motives underlying it. Domain refers to the types of government transactions and functions where corruption exists. Scale refers to the magnitude of corruption associated with specific domains. Corruption may also be categorized by the motives of bribe givers and takers.

The nature and type of corruption that occurs in government transactions tends to vary with the kind of functions and activities involved. Thus, corruption may exist in the policymaking process

---

[2] For a detailed discussion, see Raj Kumar (2011).

when public officials at the highest levels engage in the abuse of public power for private gain. This may result in the phenomenon of 'policy capture' by special interest groups such as business lobbies with whom politicians or officials may have colluded. Changes in investment, trade and tax policies, for example, could be the outcome of corrupt deals struck between public officials and certain industry lobbies.[3] At the other end of the spectrum, are a set of activities that can be termed 'public service delivery', for which a majority of the citizens depend on the government. Each transaction here may be small, but could offer much scope for corruption as millions of people, most with limited knowledge, are involved. In between these two categories, is yet another set of activities that may be called 'procurement' or the purchase of the inputs needed to implement policies and to provide the public services referred to earlier. These inputs include goods and services, human resources and technologies that the government mobilizes in order to deliver its policies and services.

The scale of corruption also matters. It is, therefore, useful to distinguish between 'grand corruption' and small-time or 'retail corruption'. Serious abuse of public power may occur in the context of what is referred to earlier as 'policy capture' by vested interests who may offer large bribes and other benefits to tilt policies in their favour. Political and bureaucratic leaders are known to fall for such grand corruption. Major scams and abuses that pertain to the allocation of scarce natural resources, large public investments and major projects also qualify as grand corruption. Small bribes paid by ordinary citizens in order to access essential public services and welfare schemes are examples of retail corruption. These bribes, though small, can add up to large sums as the victims run into millions.

---

[3] This is not to say that all such changes entail corrupt deals. If the policymaking process is transparent and complies with laid down procedures, society will accept such decisions as consistent with public interest.

Corruption, irrespective of size and form, may also be categorized by the motives that drive bribe takers and givers. When both parties perceive an act of corruption as mutually beneficial, it can be termed 'collusive'. Collusive corruption occurs when bribe takers and givers willingly agree to engage in the abuse of public power for private gain. It is a proactive effort to violate the law or subvert public interest. This is in contrast to the 'coercive' corruption encountered by an average citizen who is forced to pay bribes to minimize undue delays and harassment at the hands of public officials. She does so most reluctantly as there is no other option left. Its defining feature is extortion. Collusive corruption is more difficult to tackle than the coercive variety.

This three-way classification of corruption sheds useful light on the nature and anatomy of the corruption phenomenon. Grand corruption occurs in the context of policy capture, large investments and contracts. Retail or small-time corruption thrives in the delivery of public services on which millions of people depend. Collusion is more likely to prevail in grand corruption than in its retail counterpart. Coercion, on the other hand, is the hallmark of corruption in the delivery of public services.

Though it is not easy to marshall robust evidence on the extent and growth of corruption in India's public life, growing public dissatisfaction with and protests against corrupt practices are a warning that needs to be taken seriously by all concerned. According to media reports, the size of bribes and the magnitude of scams in monetary terms have increased manifold. Growing urbanization, the media's role in tracking and disseminating corruption stories and the power of new social media in communication and networking have significantly contributed to growing public concern about corruption.[4]

---

[4] The recent campaign of India Against Corruption led by Anna Hazare, Arvind Kejriwal and others has provided ample evidence of the power of these factors.

Why corruption is pervasive in India[5]

There are several reasons why corruption is as prevalent as it is in India.[6] First, ignorance and lack of awareness among citizens about their rights and traditional practices of paying bribes to public officials seem to have resulted in a tolerance of corruption in our society. This state of affairs has encouraged most political parties to openly distribute cash and gifts to voters during election time. Such practices continue because large segments of the population seek personal favours and benefits rather than policy shifts and system reforms from their elected representatives and other public leaders. Laws may have been passed against such practices, but many people pay scant attention to them. When political leaders, including elected representatives, do not see anything amiss in these practices, it is not surprising that they do not see controlling corruption as a priority when they come to power.

Second, the nature of the government and its functioning create scope and opportunities for corruption. Many government services are monopolistic in nature. When there is only one supplier of essential services, it becomes easy for corrupt politicians and officials to extort money or favours from those who seek the services. In recent years, efforts have been made to privatize or open up some of the services so as to introduce a measure of competition. Telecom is a fine example of this approach in India. There is intense competition among the service providers, but only the government has the power to grant telecom licences. This monopoly power lies behind the 2G and Coalgate scams. Exercising this power without transparency offers vast scope for corruption. Even when there are policies and rules to guide decisions, the use of discretion by public officials is often necessary and justified. Such discretionary decision-making within a culture of non-transparency makes it easy

[5] There are no rigorous studies on the spread and magnitude of corruption in India. Numerous studies, however, have documented the extent of corruption through surveys in different states and regions in the country. Inter-country comparisons also have rated India as highly corrupt. The Transparency International's corruption index ranked India 94th in the world in 2013.

[6] For a fuller discussion, see Paul (2013).

for public officials to favour those who are willing to give them bribes in some form or another. Corruption in the award of large contracts, allocation of scarce assets such as land, mining rights and other licences, and appointments and transfers of officials can be attributed to this feature of the functioning of the government.

Third, the abuse of public power for private gain could have been minimized if the government had the capacity and commitment to monitor its activities, policies and programmes on a regular basis. Budgets are prepared, but the norms for expenditure control and the outcomes expected from the expenditure are seldom spelt out. Holding public officials accountable for results then becomes almost impossible. The culture of systematic monitoring and evaluation of public expenditure is, by and large, weak among most governments and in their agencies. The government's activities, programmes and policies are admittedly more complex and subject to many constraints compared to those of business enterprises. The point to note here is that poorly managed and monitored public expenditure can create vast opportunities for the abuse of public power. Much of the abuses in public services stems from this failure of monitoring. Media, both print and electronic, has played a useful role by stepping in to monitor key government decisions, programmes and policies which are of public interest. But given its need to move on to other emerging issues, the media, too, fails to monitor them on a continuing basis.

Fourth, when citizens are unaware of their rights and are denied information about the terms and conditions of their transactions with governmental agencies, the delivery of essential public services can become a fertile ground for corruption. When a service provider withholds such essential information from the citizen, the latter will remain ignorant of her rights.

The provider can exploit this ignorance and extract bribes from him or her. Grievance redressal is another area where citizens may have scant information. Public officials may resort to harassment and delay tactics that may force hapless citizens to pay bribes under these conditions. There are several examples of the use of technology that could empower people with the requisite information to access public services. But progress on these reforms has been rather slow. Resistance to such reforms stems from powerful sections in government who benefit by witholding information.

These imbalances that clearly favour governments and their service providers translate into imbalances of power. They are at the heart of the inefficient and corrupt public services in India. The worst sufferers of these imbalances are the poor who have neither the power nor the resources to counter them.[7] Other factors such as lack of training of staff members and adequate resources and technology may also be responsible for the unresponsive and predatory behaviour of public officials towards ordinary citizens. But these in turn may also be linked to the indifferent attention given by political leaders and public authorities to the mutually reinforcing imbalances (asymmetries) discussed earlier. While these problems are not unique to India, what is noteworthy is that many countries have corrected these imbalances and improved access, efficiency and accountability in their public services. It is a transformation that is yet to take place in India.

Finally, the manner in which political parties are managed and the financing of national, state and local-level elections have contributed much to the spread and scale of corruption in India's public life. Political parties and candidates need large funds for fighting elections and running the party machineries between elections. There is little accountability and transparency in the collection and use of their funds, creating in the process enormous scope for generating much 'dark money' and corruption. Once unaccounted funds are deployed for elections, the winners use their power and discretion to recoup their investments and more while in power, and get ready for the next round of elections. A vicious cycle of corruption is thus created that is difficult to break. Public interest groups, the media and other activists have continually highlighted the corruption stemming from this unholy nexus among politicians, bureaucrats and businessmen. Protection of the corrupt is here to stay in the prevailing system of politics. Though politicians are

---

[7] Citizen report cards on public services published by the Public Affairs Centre, Bangalore, have shown that the burden of corruption (as a proportion of their income) is much higher for poor households than for the rest.

generally hesitant to dwell publicly on corruption issues, some political leaders have openly admitted that our political institutions are among the most corrupt. A recent example is of an icon of the young generation, Rahul Gandhi.[8]

Until the early part of the twentieth century, political systems and culture in Europe and the United States were characterized by rampant corruption. Patronage politics, sale and purchase of parliamentary seats and corruption in the awarding of contracts were common practices. India's political system and culture today are reminiscent of that age. The influence of money power and feudal leaders who control vote banks are there for all to see. A quarter or more of the MPs are known to have criminal cases against them.[9] In the west, corruption in political and administrative systems has been eliminated to a large extent due to enlightened leadership, enforcing the rule of law, eliminating conflicts of interest and greater transparency over several generations. Will India need a century or two to achieve this transformation? Can we telescope and complete the process of corruption control in our generation?

What are the barriers to corruption control?

Of the multiple causes of corruption highlighted earlier, indifference to the rule of law and lack of integrity in the political system and electoral politics have significantly contributed to the political leaders' and other policymakers' reluctance to eradicate corruption. The prevailing opaque system of financing most political parties and the lack of transparency and accountability in electoral finances leave much scope for the use of dark money and unfair and arbitrary influences on policymaking once parties come to power. It is widely believed that corrupt officials in the government who collect bribes from the people contribute to their political

---

[8] Mr Gandhi's statement on corruption before a meeting of the Youth Wing of the Congress party was reported in the *Times of India* on 29 November 2011.

[9] Reports by Election Watch (ADR) and the Public Affairs Centre have documented these facts.

protectors and parties in a big way. An opaque system that thrives on cash transactions is thus tailormade for corrupt political leaders enriching themselves. They can hardly be expected to champion the reform of this system or of fighting corruption in public life. For them and their allies in the bureaucracy, public accountability and the rule of law are low priority matters. Yet, seldom do public debates in the electronic media and writings on corruption highlight this fundamental flaw in the system. As long as this malaise persists, there is little hope of successfully containing corruption, for the simple reason that the control and oversight of public institutions and their governance are vested in political leaders. Reforms in the way political parties function and their electoral-financing practices must receive the highest priority in the fight against corruption, though it is the hardest nut to crack. The tolerance of corruption at the societal level and the inability of large sections of the people to resist corrupt practices has created an environment that poses no credible threat to corrupt political parties, elected representatives and business leaders. Re-orienting the governance system and its practices and correcting the asymmetries that render public services inefficient and corrupt are not impossible tasks.

The vicious circle created by the mutually reinforcing nature of the causal factors discussed here is not easy to break. A political system that is fed by the toxic waters of corruption and non-transparency creates a fertile ground for the perpetuation of 'patron–client relations.'[10] In this scenario, a major segment of public policies, services and regulatory approvals will be delivered to the clients in the network of money power and other influences that support or are linked to political and bureaucratic patrons.

---

[10] Patrons are, for the most part, political leaders, elected representatives and bureaucrats who exercise public power. Clients are those who seek favours, decisions and benefits of all kinds from the patrons. Both the rich and the poor can become clients who link up with patrons to obtain the benefits that they seek. Those who support the patrons with money or with organizational power for gathering votes succeed in getting into successful patron–client relations. Caste and community loyalties play a major role in patron–client relations, especially in the context of elections at all levels.

Conflicts of interest involving policymakers will be tolerated to the detriment of public interest. Reforms in the administrative and service delivery systems and practices that may benefit society at large will be low priority as these will put roadblocks in the working of patron–client relations. This also explains why many laws are passed, but are not enforced or are made toothless. It tells us why those responsible for implementing major policies, schemes and regulations are not held accountable for their performance. Resistance to reforms in the political party and the electoral financing system, reluctance to abolish patron–client relations, undue delays in passing several anti-corruption bills pending in Parliament and neglecting systemic reforms to make service delivery and the functioning of public institutions more open, effective and responsive to the public at large are closely intertwined. There is no lack of knowledge about e-governance and other reforms that can make public services, procurement and regulatory processes corruption free. It is the fear that they will strike at the root of clientilism, patronage and political funding that causes resistance to change in responsible quarters. These linkages and the vicious circle that they create are at the heart of the problem of corruption. The end result is that people lose trust in the government.

It is important to remind ourselves that there are no quick fixes to successfully tackling corruption. The problem calls for a multi-pronged approach, combining reforms at different levels, strategies for eliciting the support of all the relevant stakeholders and persistent public campaigns. The remedy needs to go beyond enacting laws and punitive measures to punish the guilty, focusing also on preventive measures that can reduce the scope and opportunities for corruption in public life. It is instructive to recall that the importance of taking preventive measures to tackle corruption was emphasized by the Santhanam Committee on Corruption almost 50 years ago in 1964. The first Administrative Reforms Commission had recommended creating the Lok Pal and Lok Ayukta institutions in 1966. But the will and sense of urgency to take follow-up actions are sadly missing in the political leadership. This is clearly brought out by a close look at what happened to the anti-corruption proposals made in the past few decades by the government's various official committees.

Mechanisms to prevent, monitor and punish corruption in India are not adequate nor have they proved to be effective to the extent that they exist. At the national level, the Parliament passed a bill to create the institution of the Lok Pal (national ombudsman) to deal with corruption among ministers and the higher bureaucracy only in December 2013.[11] In general, governments at the Centre and in the states have been tardy at best, and insincere at worst, in investigating and pursuing corruption. Commissions of inquiry established over the years have not been able to effectively prove or penalize corruption. Corruption has been politicized—just as politics has been corrupted – in the sense that cases of corruption have often been used for partisan political purposes, rather than with any serious intent to objectively tackle the problem.

The low priority given to controlling corruption masks a variety of factors. Vested interests that benefit from corruption will certainly put roadblocks to kill plans for reforms. The silence of the majority may be read as people's indifference by those in authority. The complex nature of some of the measures presented here may make consensus-building a long-drawn-out process. Populist policies and schemes may leave no time or resources with the powers that be to pursue the cause of controlling corruption. There are those in the government who champion economic reforms, poverty alleviation, environment, defence and the like. But there is no champion in the government or strong and durable lobbies outside it for fighting corruption. When the gains from controlling corruption are widely diffused among millions of people across a vast country, each of whom benefits only in an imperceptible manner, the incentive for them to fight corruption is rather weak. The beneficiaries of corruption, on the other hand, are a small sub-set of this large population, but well organized and interlinked. Political parties, bureaucrats and middlemen make significant gains

[11] The first Lok Pal bill was introduced in Parliament 46 years ago! Many versions of the bill have been debated on over decades with no consensus to get it passed, a clear case of lack of political will.

from corruption, and hence they have a much stronger incentive to preserve the status quo.[12]

What is the way forward?

As noted earlier, there is no lack of knowledge in government circles about the action to be taken for controlling corruption. Improved service delivery alone can reduce the scope for corruption and harassment of ordinary citizens. Vague rules, absence of deadlines for service delivery and unwarranted bureaucratic discretion can cause much harassment and delays that hurt ordinary citizens, leaving them no option but to submit themselves to extortion. Introducing a better designed system with transparent and clear-cut procedures may well reduce the scope for such corruption. Several governments have taken such remedial action with positive results. If all public agencies and departments were to take steps to simplify procedures for getting essential services, provide information proactively to citizens to empower them to access the services and improve the system for monitoring service delivery, it will not only enhance efficiency, but will also help control corruption. The Right to Services Act is an example of a reform along these lines. It remains to be seen whether it will be implemented by the states as planned. Governments could promote e-governance to make services more efficient and accountability stronger. They could seek citizen feedback on services as a means of improving officials' quality and responsiveness. Regulatory agencies can be made more independent and their decisions made known with speed and transparency. Websites can be used to usher in greater transparency and timeliness. Take the widespread practice of delayed payments by government departments and agencies to contractors and even other public institutions that have completed works entrusted to them. It is an open secret that involved officials

---

[12] This is not to say that all politicians and bureaucrats are corrupt. However, powerful groups among them who actually engage in corruption can derail reforms and successfully maintain the status quo.

demand bribes to cut the delays that they had created in the first place. Remedies for this systemic problem are readily available, yet no one in the government has taken the lead to eliminate this abominable practice. The same applies to political parties which, with the aid of technology, can disclose details of their sources of funds and donations, even if they are small. A new political party, the Aam Aadmi Party (AAP) has shown how this can be done with ease. None of these steps call for huge resources or unusual expertise. But those who champion single-point programmes to fight corruption should note that little will be accomplished without wide-ranging reforms.

A major reform that will call for substantial resources is the public funding of elections, which is the only way to minimize the evil influence of dark money on the political system. Political parties are often hesitant to take this route for cleansing election finances as they argue that this is a costly proposition. But the additional funds required can be reduced if the Members of Parliament Local Area Development (MPLADS) and other schemes of dubious value can be pruned. Given this scenario, the government's failure to act can be attributed to only one reason: a lack of political will. There is no reason to believe that a paradigm shift is about to occur to move us towards corruption-free governance in the near future.

It is against this backdrop that we need to consider the critical role that civil society needs to play. Civil society organizations will have to play the role of a proactive watchdog by monitoring, exposing and protesting abuse of power, corruption and other illegal and unethical acts committed by governments and their agencies. They can propose policy alternatives and adopt new ways to fight corruption and improve governance and accountability. They have a vital role to play in enhancing citizens' awareness about their rights and their willingness and ability to resist corrupt practices. Admittedly, these are not easy tasks to perform, and it is an uphill task for civil society organizations to sustain public interest in these issues for long periods for the reasons explained earlier. There are many civil society groups which are striving to play this proactive role in India against heavy odds. There are others that have fallen by the wayside.

As against these limitations, there are some positive developments that can aid civil society in its fight against corruption. New technologies are now available that can assist civic groups to mobilize and stimulate citizens to come together and engage in collective action. The use of social media for this purpose in recent anti-corruption campaigns is a case in point. Networking has become far easier now, especially in urban areas, reinforced by rising educational levels and public anger against corruption. Civic groups are increasingly using social accountability tools and community engagement to demand better governance. Social audits, citizen report cards on public services, public interest litigations and public hearings are examples of such tools. They can be used to exert citizen pressure on public agencies to be more accountable and responsive. The Right to Information Act (RTI) has become a widely used instrument for exposing and fighting corruption. The higher judiciary and constitutional bodies such as the Election Commission and the Comptroller and Auditor General of India (CAG) are playing a key role in challenging abuses of power and corruption. The media's active role in the dissemination of news and investigative journalism is also a positive trend. An agile civil society that can take advantage of these developments and engage in collective action to challenge the state to deliver corruption-free governance is the mark of a vibrant democracy. It is only when significant numbers of people signal to the political parties and governments that they will not tolerate corruption that the needed political will to reform the system of governance will emerge.

Anti-corruption reforms, briefly referred to earlier, call for changes in multiple dimensions of governance: policymaking, regulatory systems, organizational structures, service delivery and the functioning of the judicial and legal systems. A common feature of these reforms is that none of them can be achieved without the initiative and commitment of the central and state governments. As pointed out earlier, there are many barriers that make this an uphill task. Apart from civic groups, other key stakeholders such as the media and industry also need to be proactive in pressing for urgent action. Though some of the leaders of industry speak out on this issue, concerted efforts on their part have been few and far between. A specific initiative that concerned corporates could launch is a fund for an independent social audit of the huge expenditures incurred by governments for numerous programmes and projects. Governments are generally reluctant to evaluate these expenditures and their impacts. Independent assessments by credible third parties based on the feedback from people will not only be a source of learning but will also act as an effective means for spotting areas of corruption and inefficiency.[13] If leaders of industry pool together a tenth of the amount that they allocate to meeting their corporate social responsibility (CSR) for supporting independent and professional assessments of the kind mentioned earlier, and publicize the results, it can have a salutary effect on both governance and corruption in public life. Credible organizations are essential for conducting and sustaining these exercises. Creating this platform will call for careful coordination and commitment of resources, but it is certainly doable. It is an intervention that could give 'voice' to the people and nudge those in authority to improve the quality of governance and bring corruption under control.

Fighting corruption will be a long-drawn-out struggle for all those committed to this cause. There will be light at the end of the tunnel only when citizens' demand for accountable governance reaches its tipping point and India's culture of feudal politics gives way to a genuinely people-centred democracy.

References

Collier, Paul. (2007). *The Bottom Billion: Why the Poorest Countries are Failing and What Can be Done About It.* New York: Oxford University Press.

---

[13] The Public Affairs Centre in Bangalore has done many such social audits and citizen report cards, but corporate or other funding for such efforts has been minimal. The importance of independent assessments is yet to be appreciated by the corporate world and many of our intellectuals. A positive development is that at least some governments have begun to commission such service delivery audits.

HM Government. (2010). *UK Bribery Act 2010.* London: HM Government.

Klitgaard, Robert. (1988). *Controlling Corruption.* Berkeley: University of California Press.

OECD. (1997). *Convention on Combating Bribery of Foreign Public Officials in International Business Transactions.* Paris: OECD.

Paul, Samuel (ed.). (2013). *Fighting Corruption: The Way Forward.* New Delhi: Academic Foundation.

Raj Kumar, C. (2011). *Corruption and Human Rights in India.* New Delhi: Oxford University Press.

Chapter 7

Corporate Governance: Issues and Challenges

T.T. Ram Mohan

It is more than two decades since the movement for corporate governance gathered momentum worldwide. It is worth asking what it has achieved and what remains to be done. The short answer is that in terms of putting in place processes and structures that could contribute to better governance, a great deal has happened. And yet the outcomes intended, greater accountability to shareholders and to society at large, remain elusive.

A certain cynicism has crept into the debate on corporate governance. There is a sense that, as with corruption or equity, it is something that people will keep talking about without anything substantive happening on the ground. As in many other areas, politics will trump economics, that is, the power of vested interests will ensure that reforms leading to better performance will not happen.

In what follows, we lay out the fundamental issues in governance, the governance problem and the mechanisms of governance. We then explore the reality with respect to governance and attempts at reforms in the Anglo-Saxon world. We move on to the Indian situation, taking in our stride the framework for governance until recently and the statute enacted in 2013.

We argue that what has passed for governance reforms is unlikely to succeed because it is no more than tinkering at the edges or tokenism. Nor can governance be left entirely to 'market forces'. We need a bolder, more radical approach to governance that takes its cues from bank regulation and relies on more intrusive regulation as an instrument of board-room reforms.

The governance objective and issues in corporate governance

Corporate governance is, very simply, the entire set of legal and institutional mechanisms designed to achieve the basic objective of a company (Sarkar and Sarkar 2012. This section and the next draw upon the exposition in chapter 1 of the book). This raises the question: 'What is the basic objective of a company?'

The objective that has been found to be operationally convenient is: maximization of shareholder value over the long-run. The insertion of 'long-run' in the statement is important. It implies that decisions taken by the management may not appear to maximize shareholder value at any given point in time but would do so when a longer time horizon is considered.

There are those who believe that maximizing shareholder wealth is too narrow an objective or that it does not capture the management's responsibilities towards other constituents of a company such as employees, customers, vendors and suppliers. The alternative proposed is the 'stakeholder' perspective.

Here, a balance is sought to be struck among the different constituencies. While this sounds more exalted in principle, it is difficult to operationalize. It is possible, for instance, for managers to justify low returns to equity on the ground that they are striving for the greater good of customers or suppliers! Investors end up lacking a criterion for judging performance.

A more sensible approach is the one that tries to reconcile the two perspectives by saying that there is no fundamental conflict between them. Managers may focus on maximizing shareholder value as long as they adhere to laws and norms that apply to other constituents, namely, labour laws, consumer protection codes and environmental legislation.

Suppose we accept that the objective is maximizing shareholder wealth. What precisely is the governance problem? The problem arises because of the separation of ownership from control. If a company is fully owned and run by the owner himself, there is no governance issue. However, in a typical Anglo-Saxon public limited company, shareholders invest in the company and entrust its management to professionals. The governance challenge is aligning the interests of the management with those of the shareholders.

This challenge is not easily met because it is difficult for the owners to write 'perfect contracts' for managers, that is, contracts that cover every possible situation in which they are required to take decisions. In these situations, we have what is called a 'principal–agent' problem. The principal, the shareholder, cannot closely monitor the actions and decisions of the agent, the manager. The alignment of interests is sought to be brought about with the help of both internal and external mechanisms, which we now elaborate upon.

The need for aligning interests arises under two very different situations. One, shareholders are widely dispersed (Type I). Here, there is potential for managers to do what they please because shareholders are not cohesive enough to exert control.

Two, there is a concentration of shareholding and the principal shareholder is also a part of the management (Type II). Examples of this are companies controlled by industrial houses or public sector enterprises, as in India. Here, conflicts can arise between the dominant shareholder and the minority shareholders. Minority shareholders may be expropriated by the majority shareholder. If the majority shareholder has a less than 50 per cent stake, he has an incentive to siphon off funds because the bigger portion of the cost will be borne by shareholders other than himself.

Corporate governance mechanisms

Corporate governance involves internal mechanisms, external mechanisms and an appropriate institutional framework. It is useful to review these in brief.

Internal mechanisms

Internal mechanisms are:

i. Board of directors: In theory, the board is the principal internal mechanism for safeguarding the interests of shareholders, whether dispersed shareholders (Type I) or minority shareholders (Type II). The board appoints and removes the CEO, monitors his performance, ensures the integrity of the accounts presented to shareholders as well as compliance with laws and regulations.

ii. Large shareholders: Retail shareholders are a relatively small component of the class of shareholders. Most savings are routed through institutional shareholders such as mutual funds, pension funds, insurance companies and hedge funds. Institutions can bring their voting powers to bear on the management. This is called 'institutional activism'.

iii. Activism on the part of institutions contrasts with the earlier policy of institutions where they preferred to 'vote with their feet', that is, by selling shares in the company. There is a sense that simply exiting a non-performing company may not suffice for institutional investors for two reasons. One, it is not easy for large shareholders to exit quickly without causing a steep drop in price and incurring the concomitant costs. Two, by the time institutions come to the conclusion that the stock is not worth holding on to, the price has already fallen steeply.

iv. Financial structure: There is a case for having a certain amount of debt in any company. The argument is that if there is too much of 'free cash' with managers, they will be tempted to 'fool' around with it. In other words, debt acts as a disciplining device by pre-empting excess free cash with managers.

v. Performance-linked incentives: Variable pay linked to performance has come to be favoured as a mechanism for aligning managers' interests with those of the shareholders. This seems unexceptionable in principle but, in practice, it gives rise to a number of issues. How is performance to be measured? How do we determine rewards for a given level of performance?

External mechanisms

Aligning managerial performance with shareholder interests can happen through a variety of external mechanisms as well:

i. Stock price: The ups and downs of stock prices are monitored by analysts and investors. They invite comments from various constituents of a company, including its board and shareholders. The stock price can thus act as a disciplining device.

ii. Takeovers: A fall in stock price caused by under-performance could lead to a firm being taken over by a fresh set of investors (which could be another company). The acquiring company, which sees potential for improving the stock price, will then replace the management. Thus, the threat of takeover keeps the management on its toes.

Institutional framework

Both internal and external mechanisms can work, that is, act as disciplining devices only within a robust institutional framework. The elements of such a framework are:

i. Legal environment: Without effective laws and their enforcement, corporate governance cannot be effective. Debt can discipline the management only if the laws provide for recovery of debts on time. Shareholders' and debt-holders' claims can be enforced only if there are bankruptcy laws that work.

ii. Political economy: How laws are framed and enforced is a matter of political economy. If business interests can subvert laws and regulation, corporate governance is reduced to nought.

iii. Accounting and disclosure norms: The performance of the management can be monitored only if a company's accounts are disclosed correctly and in a timely manner. This requires norms for the auditing profession as well as norms for accounting and disclosure and enforcing these norms.

Corporate governance realities

It should be evident that an elaborate paraphernalia for governance is in place in terms of both internal and external mechanisms needed to discipline the management. And yet there is profound discomfort about the state of governance not just in emerging markets but in developed economies as well. Scandals in the corporate world involving the collapse of large companies such as Enron and WorldCom in the non-financial sector as also the more recent failures in banking in the sub-prime crisis suggest that something is rotten in the state of corporate governance. There are at least four areas in which corporate governance has not lived up to expectations.

One area is lack of reliability of accounts. This has been symbolized by high-profile cases such as Enron in the US and Satyam in India. A second area of concern is ineffective boards. Although the CEO is nominally responsible to the board and answerable to it, often it is the board that tends to be dominated by the CEO.

A third problem is autocratic CEOs whose whimsical ways have led to the collapse of big companies. This problem again arises because of diffused shareholders and ineffective boards. It is often suggested that corporations are made or unmade by CEOs. Whether this is inevitable or desirable—whether performance should centre around one so-called 'leader'—needs to be seriously questioned.

Finally, executive salaries have been the subject of much controversy not just amongst shareholders but among regulators and policymakers as well. Outsized packages are sought to be justified on the grounds of aligning managerial incentives with shareholder interests. All too often, however, managerial pay acquires a life of its own. Top management virtually sets its own pay, including hefty severance packages, and the link between pay and performance is tenuous at best.

The response to these issues of governance has been two-fold. One, as noted earlier, is introducing norms for stricter compliance and disclosure, as exemplified by the Sarbannes-Oxley Act and the creation of an oversight authority for auditors in the US. The other response, which has happened in many other parts of the world, is strengthening the boards through appointing 'independent' directors, that is, directors from outside a company who are expected to monitor management.

A related move is constituting sub-committees of the board such as audit, remuneration and nomination committees with responsibilities for accounts, executive compensations and selecting independent directors respectively. Independent directors are expected to have an important role in these sub-committees.

However, the induction of independent directors has, by and large, not made a significant difference to the effectiveness of boards. It is not hard to see why. In principle, an Anglo-Saxon corporation represents a 'shareholders' democracy' where owners of equity are supposed to elect their nominees to the board.

In practice, given that the shareholding is diffused, the management chooses the board members. We thus have a rather quixotic situation where the management selects the board and the board selects the management. In such a situation, how the board is expected to act independently is a mystery.

The corporate governance problem in India

India mostly faces the Type II governance problem mentioned at the beginning of this essay, namely, the risk of expropriation of the minority shareholder by the majority shareholder. In the Anglo-Saxon model, professionally managed firms dominate the universe of listed firm. In India, listed firms (which are also among the larger firms) have one of three forms of dominant owners: family business, government and multinational corporations (MNCs) (Varma 1997). Professionally managed firms such as Infosys and Larsen & Toubro are relatively rare and even some of these have tended to assume the qualities of 'promoter' companies.

Given that the dominant owner has a significant stake (anywhere in the range of 30–50 per cent for corporate houses and even higher in the case of public sector undertakings and MNCs), it would appear that there is a natural alignment between the management's interests (which represent the dominant shareholder) and performance. However, while the management may not act in ways that are detrimental to the interests of the dominant shareholder, it could certainly act in ways that are detrimental to the interests of the minority shareholder. This can happen for various reasons in each category of dominant owners.

In a family business, where the family has an equity stake of, say 30 per cent, the dominant owner has an obvious interest in siphoning off funds. For any ₹100 lost to the company, the loss to the dominant owner is only ₹30; the bigger portion of the loss, ₹70, is borne by institutional and retail shareholders. One of the virtues of rapid growth is that it diminishes such incentives for siphoning funds out of the company. This is because rapid growth translates into a rise in market capitalization of companies. The owner stands to gain more by encashing his shares in a rapidly growing company than by taking funds out of the company.

In public sector undertakings (PSUs), conflict can arise between the dominant owner, the government and other shareholders because the government often acts in ways that are contrary to the maximization of shareholder value. The government may want a PSU to make investments in the larger interests of the economy. It may want PSUs to invest in places that have vote-catching possibilities for politicians in power.

Again, the government may compel PSUs to acquire equity in other PSUs or to pay large dividends merely in order to bridge the budgetary deficit (familiar enough in the present context). It may under-price PSU products in the larger public interest. All these concerns have been the subject of public discourse in India ever since PSUs came to be listed.

MNCs, one would suppose, are the torch-bearers of governance as they are expected to bring superior global practices into the country. We now know better. A few questionable practices may be mentioned by way of illustration.

One is the transfer of high-value brands from a subsidiary in which a MNC has a relatively low stake to a subsidiary in which the MNC has a 100 per cent stake. If the transfer is priced on terms that benefit the latter, minority shareholders in the former clearly lose out. Another is the practice of charging 'brand royalty' for products sold in India. This results, in effect, in the parent receiving a higher dividend than other shareholders. A third cause for concern is transfer pricing of transactions between the parent MNC and its local subsidiary. This can happen in ways that cause a loss not only to Indian shareholders but also to Indian tax authorities.

India thus faces a set of governance challenges that are rather different from the ones associated with the Anglo-Saxon world. Ours is, in general, the Type II governance problem rather than the Type I governance problem.

The corporate governance framework in India

The corporate governance framework in India and also attempts at reforms have been patterned on those in the Anglo-Saxon model despite the fact that the underlying governance problem in India, as pointed out earlier, is rather different.

In India, the corporate governance framework has thus far rested on Clause 49 of the listing agreement with the stock exchanges. More recently, the Companies Act (2013) has brought corporate governance within the framework of the statute (with some of its requirements departing from those under Clause 49).

Some of the principal features of Clause 49 are:

- One-third of the board should comprise independent directors. If the chairman is an executive or belongs to the promoter group, half of the board should comprise independent directors.
- The board should have an audit committee that examines and approves the company's accounts and appoints the company's auditors. This committee should have a minimum of three members with two-thirds of the members being independent directors.
- There are no mandatory requirements for constituting a remuneration committee to fix compensation for the top management or a nomination committee to select board members and to appoint the CEO. Many boards have opted to have these on their own. However, there is a requirement for a section in the annual report that documents governance practices and spells out compensation for the top management as well as independent and non-executive directors.
- There are norms for disclosure of related party transactions.

Clause 49 fulfilled the need for norms for corporate governance which were not covered under the Companies Act. The Companies Act (2013), however, addresses this lacuna in the statutes and moves to strengthen corporate governance in several ways:

- It has provisions for constituting nomination and remuneration committees in addition to the audit committee of the board. Both these committees must have a minimum of three non-executive directors of whom at least half must be independent directors.

- It provides for rotation of auditor firms every 10 years, with individual auditors being allowed to stay on for a maximum of five years.
- It limits the total number of directorships held by an individual to 20, out of which not more than 10 can be in public limited companies.
- It introduces the concept of an independent director in the Companies Act and mandates that one-third of the board should be independent directors.
- It limits the term of an independent director to two terms of five years each, something that is not covered by Clause 49.
- It disallows giving stock options to independent directors. They can be paid only a sitting fee and commission.
- It provides for evaluation of independent directors and the board as a whole.

The Companies Act (2013) is a step forward as it brings corporate governance within the scope of the statutes. However, some infirmities in the provisions are apparent. These reflect compromises made in order to appease business interests, again a case of politics trumping economics.

Independent directors, who have served for 10 years, may be re-appointed after a hiatus of three years. Moreover, the 10-year term will apply subsequent to the passing of the act; the period sent by serving independent directors prior to the passing of the act is not to be counted. This is absurd. After all, the principle underlying fixed terms for independent directors is that their independence is compromised when they are associated with a company for too long.

Moreover, anyone who has sat on a board will readily concede that it is hard to justify a director's holding 10 directorships at a time in public limited companies (or in any category of company, for that matter). It would be more appropriate to limit the number of independent directorships to five (a proposal that is said to be under SEBI's consideration for inclusion in Clause 49).

The nomination and remuneration committees have been given responsibility for setting compensation. It is not clear, however, whether the basis for compensation is to be disclosed in the annual report or not. This is the one question in executive pay that defies understanding: how does the board arrive at a particular package for the CEO and other senior executives in a given year?

Then, with respect to the evaluation of independent directors and the board, who is the evaluation to be shared with? Unless specifics relating to these issues are squarely addressed and resolved, corporate governance may continue to be an exercise in just ticking boxes.

These infirmities apart, there is a fundamental flaw in both Clause 49 and the relevant provisions of the Companies Act (2013). This is the presumption governance reforms are all about mimicking the Anglo-Saxon proposals for the constitution of the board.

We have seen earlier in this essay that boards are ineffective even in the Anglo-Saxon system where ownership is diffused and equities are owned predominantly by an assortment of institutional investors. Where ownership is concentrated, as in India, there is even more reason to expect that the board will end up as a handmaiden of the dominant owner, be it a corporate house or the Government of India.

The board is constituted by the dominant owner (often called the 'promoter'). 'Independent' directors are chosen by the dominant owner. Management is the dominant owner himself or again it is appointed by the dominant owner. The idea that in such a scheme of things, the board can be expected to act in the interests of minority shareholders is hardly credible. The more likely outcome is that the dominant owner will call the shots through the mechanism of the board.

In recent years, we have seen corporate India inducting retired bureaucrats, bankers and regulators as independent directors, often on handsome terms. This is bound to signal to those in positions of authority that if they deal favourably with the companies in question, they can expect to be rewarded on retirement.

Again, we can see how politics trumps economics. The mechanism of independent directors is intended to improve corporate governance. Instead, it may have had the perverse effect of worsening the governance problem in a broader sense.

Some radical proposals for improving corporate governance in India

Boards of directors have shown themselves unable to pose hard questions and taking tough decisions needed to safeguard the interests of shareholders. They have not done a good job either of other key board functions such as planning successions, setting transparent norms for compensation for top executives and ensuring diversity in the boards.

We need to breathe life into the architecture of governance in which the board is the key element. It is often contended that more capital market discipline is the answer to the governance problem in India. If this were true, we would not be seeing the aberrations that we have in markets that are far more efficient than ours and which have a superior record of institutional activism.

No, market forces cannot provide all the answer to the governance problem in any context. We need more stringent regulations to ensure that boards perform. In India, the regulations under the aegis of Clause 49 or the Companies Act (2013) need to be significantly modified. In drawing up an appropriate set of regulations for governance, it would be useful to draw upon the experience of bank regulations, as they obtain in India and also the evolving set of bank regulations elsewhere.

In what follows, we outline some radical proposals for reforms in corporate governance, drawing on the experience of bank regulation in some instances.

Board composition and selection

In India, the RBI prescribes a certain desired composition of the board, namely, that it should include an economist, a person with banking experience, somebody with expertise in the small and medium enterprises sector, and so on. It has laid down 'fit and proper' criteria for membership of banks' boards. In the UK, the Financial Services Authority (FSA) interviews candidates proposed for the boards of financial firms. In some cases, it asks for candidates to be withdrawn. It may be appropriate to institute these norms for non-financial companies as well, at least for companies above a certain size to start with.

But we need to go well beyond these prescriptions. We need to tackle the fundamental problem with boards head-on: the unwillingness of boards to question and challenge the management. We need truly independent boards, that is, directors who are not beholden to the management (or the dominant owner) for their appointments. For this to happen, the selection of board members itself must be independent of the management (or the dominant owner).

We need to rethink the norms for selecting independent directors. It is necessary that a variety of stakeholders be represented on the board. To begin with, we must mandate that the dominant owner can choose a maximum of 50 per cent of independent directors.

The remaining independent directors must come from other stakeholders: institutional shareholders, minority shareholders, employees, and perhaps, civil society as well. If necessary, the number of independent directors can be increased beyond the one-third mandated by the Companies Act (2013) so that there is broad-based representation on the board.

Corporate India often talks of a 'scarcity' of qualified people to sit on boards. What it means is that it cannot find people outside a closed club that comprises present and former CEOs or senior executives, retired bureaucrats, chartered accountants with close links to the management and, of late, a few high-profile academics from abroad.

It is a mistake to think that exceptional talent or accomplishments are required to be effective on the board. Expertise about an industry or corporate performance is useful at the margins. However, boards can seldom be more knowledgeable about a company than its own management. They cannot add much value in terms of broad strategy or operational performance.

Where the board can add value is in stepping back from the minutiae of everyday performance and asking questions that challenge the management. Why are we losing market share? How is it that so many senior people are leaving? What are we doing to foster innovation? Is a succession plan in place? And so on.

We do not need 'eminence' in board members to pose these questions. Nor does asking these questions and scrutinizing the answers require extraordinary expertise. Posing the hard questions in the board-room needs commitment—and a willingness to express oneself freely.

Such commitment and independence are, of course, rare but one must expect that they are distributed equally at all levels in society. A college principal or a university professor, the head of a NGO, a retired senior banker from a public sector bank, lawyers and chartered accountants, journalists of stature—any of these are, in principle, competent to serve on a company's board.

In order to have independence, we need genuine diversity in the board, not the group-think that the current composition of most boards foster. And diversity can happen only when different stakeholders are represented by individuals drawn from different walks of life.

Board effectiveness

If we want boards to perform, we must be able to monitor their effectiveness. Here again, there are useful lessons to be drawn from bank regulations.

The FSA has made a number of proposals on this subject:

- An externally-facilitated review of the effectiveness of the board should be conducted every two years and the outcome of the review should be discussed by the chairman with the bank's FSA supervisor. The Companies Act (2013), proposes an evaluation of board members but does not propose mechanisms for doing this. One way could be for peers on the board to review each other and the chairman, with the outcomes being assessed by the regulator (SEBI) or by an outside committee appointed by the board. UK's Parliamentary Commission on Banking Standards (2013) wants to go further. It wants a designated senior independent director to evaluate the performance of the chairman and explain to the regulator how the chairman has held the

CEO to account and encouraged 'meaningful challenge' from other independent directors. It wants the chairman of a bank to hold annual meetings with heads of all sub-committees so that he or she has a comprehensive view of what is going on in the sub-committees.

- The regulator must go through the minutes and judge whether the management's proposals have been adequately debated by the board. In India, the RBI does go through the minutes of board meetings and conveys its impressions informally or in the annual financial inspection report. Lack of detailed minutes is an important lacuna in the functioning of boards.
- Major proposals for acquisitions should be evaluated by an independent advisor appointed by the board.

To begin with, SEBI may consider implementing these proposals for companies with assets above a certain size.

Executive pay

There has been a serious attempt to lay down regulations for executive pay in banking as it has come to be viewed as a source of systemic risk. One important move has been to insist that variable pay be in the form of stock options (instead of cash) whose vesting is deferred over a long period. This is to ensure that incentives are linked to long-term performance. Another move, within the European Union, has been to fix a norm of 1:1 for variable to fixed pay, which can be raised to 2:1 with shareholders' approval.

In India, CEO compensation in private banks has to be approved by the RBI. The RBI has some internal norms that link pay levels to asset size and the peer group of banks. RBI has, in some cases, asked for pay packets to be pruned when proposals were put to it for approval.

There is a case for regulating executive pay in the interests of shareholders and in the long-term interests of the firm, given the perception that executive pay in India has tended to be hijacked by the top management and has got divorced from performance.

It has also led to staggering inequalities within companies, which are unconscionable in the Indian context. One or two ideas are worth considering.

Deferring variable pay over a long period has much to commend itself as true performance is known only over a long period. Secondly, there has to be full disclosure of the basis on which boards arrive at the compensation, both fixed and variable. Although this appears to be mandated by Clause 49, such disclosure is absent in annual reports. It may also be desirable to set a ratio of the maximum and minimum pay within the top management, if not for the company as a whole. This appears necessary as the CEO's pay does appear disproportionate in relation to that of executives, even those who are one or two levels below him.

Dominance of the CEO

In the sub-prime crisis, one of the features of many failed banks was the dominance of the CEO and the absence of any challenge to the CEO from the board as well as the ranks of senior management. This was certainly one of the features that FSA noticed in the failure of the Royal Bank of Scotland.

This should not come as a big surprise. Modern corporations sit uneasily with the values of a liberal society. While a liberal society cherishes and celebrates democracy, most corporations tend to be despotisms where the writ of the CEO runs unchallenged. This is an issue that greatly troubled management thinker Peter Drucker. He expended a great deal of effort in trying to see how power in the corporation could be decentralized.

One of Drucker's ideas was that the CEO should be viewed not as a person but as a team of three, with important decisions being taken by the team and not by an individual. This may appear utopian if only because such a model is rarely to be found. But the underlying idea, namely, that there should be checks and balances on the exercise of power by the CEO needs to be squarely addressed in the interests of better governance. No individual, however accomplished, is competent to make all the important decisions in a large, modern corporation. It is only through an active contest of ideas that the best decisions are made.

If this is understood, then it is important that the board is mindful of its responsibility of ensuring that the CEO does not become overly domineering. Is there adequate delegation of powers down the line? Are senior appointments meritocratic and made in accordance with certain norms? Are performance incentives handed out to senior executives based on clearly defined criteria? Does the CEO encourage differing points of view and even active dissent?

One way to get the answers is for the board to find time to interact with managers at least up to three levels below the CEO. Another is to put in place succession plans that identify a range of possible contenders; the CEO then knows clearly that he will have to step down some day and that one of the contenders could put his actions under scrutiny.

Concluding remarks

Corporate governance is intended to ensure that corporations that often manage vast resources work in the interests of the shareholders. Most attempts at reforms in other parts of the world in recent years have tended to focus on strengthening the role of the board. This, however, may not amount to much without greater regulatory interventions. In India, reforms in corporate governance have had the effect of creating forms of governance without making a difference to content.

The evolution of bank regulation, especially since the sub-prime crisis, provides useful pointers to reforms needed in corporate governance. Regulation must focus on the composition of boards, how board members are selected, the effectiveness of boards, executive pay and checking the dominance of the CEO. Without stronger regulations, corporate governance may remain an elusive will-o'-the-wisp.

References

FSA. (2011). *The failure of the Royal Bank of Scotland*. Financial Services Authority Board report. Available at the FSA website.

Parliamentary Commission on Banking Standards. (2013). *Changing banking for good*. Available at the UK Parliament website.

Sarkar, Jayati and Subrata Sarkar. (2012). *Corporate Governance in India*. New Delhi: Sage Publications

Varma, J.R. (1997). 'Corporate governance in India: disciplining the dominant shareholder', *IIMB Management Review*, October–December 1997.

Chapter 8

Governing for an Inclusive Growth

Pulapre Balakrishnan

Introduction

This essay addresses the challenge of delivering social justice in India today and argues that this lies mainly in being able to govern the polity towards that end, that is, the delivery of social justice. Social justice itself is interpreted as the expansion of opportunities with respect to economic, educational and social development. Such an idea of justice is intuitive, capacious and amenable to realization through social policy; the last is a particularly important consideration. In the context of a growing economy, this definition of justice anticipates the criterion of inclusive growth, that is, how widespread the benefits of growth are in terms of the economic opportunities being made available. Evidence that India's political class views satisfying this criterion as important to its calculations may be seen in the centrality given to inclusive growth in the manifesto of the United Progressive Alliance (UPA), especially of the Congress party, which governed India for a decade since 2004. In fact, the Congress party has succeeded in making this intrinsic to much of the political discourse in the country today. The success of the Aam Aadmi Party (AAP) in elections to the Delhi assembly in December 2013 may be seen as the case for inclusion having been taken to the next level with concerns of ordinary Indians becoming the very rationale of the party.

This essay is arranged as follows: first, it considers how the nation's political class has shaped the public perception of inclusive growth. It then discusses appropriate criteria for judging whether growth is inclusive and proposes a strategy for attaining such growth. Finally, it characterizes the nature of the challenge faced by the project of advancing social inclusion in India today.

The political class on growth and social justice

In a democracy, the political leadership plays a key role in shaping perceptions of the country's economic and political development and the means by which this is to be advanced. In this section I provide a short account of how India's political class has set the agenda for social justice in recent times.

A decade and a half into the reforms that liberalized its trade and industrial policy regime, India is at the top of the league of fast-growing economies in the world. However, it is now officially acknowledged that this growth has not been sufficiently inclusive. Accordingly, the goal of inclusion was explicitly entered in the 'Approach' (see Planning Commission 2006) to the Eleventh Five Year Plan, for the period 2007–12. No criterion was been offered, though, by which we can judge a growth process for its inclusiveness. There is instead only a suggestion in the document that the route to inclusiveness is via a higher rate of growth. This view of the relationship between growth and social justice is explicit in official pronouncements made by the architects of the reforms from time to time. Thus, we have the following statement by Prime Minister Manmohan Singh: 'India needs to grow at the rate of at least 10 per cent per annum to get rid of chronic poverty,

ignorance and disease which still afflicts millions of our people.'[1]
To this the following statement by his then Finance Minister
P. Chidambaram may be added: 'India must touch a 10 per cent
growth and sustain it for 10, 20 and 30 years to make poverty
part of India's history.' The minister went on to say that growth
was not an end in itself but a strategy to 'raise resources and
acquire the capacity to spend more money on the provision of
goods and services that will mitigate the hardship of millions of
poor people and bring some cheer in their lives.'[2] Significantly,
this was part of the finance minister's speech in Singapore on the
rationale of the economic policies of his government. Both these
statements were issued in 2008 as 'UPA 1' was coming to the
end of its tenure and preparing for elections, and therefore, may
be taken to be in line with the Congress party's manifesto. They
may be taken to represent the political leadership's view on the
role of economic growth in advancing inclusion. They convey the
idea of growth making it possible for the government to provide
greater welfare rather than of a growth process drawing in an
increasing number via employment generation and entrepreneurial
opportunities. Arguably, it is the latter version that accords more
with a democratic definition of inclusive growth. Not captured
in these excerpts from speeches by leading political actors of that
time, but often stated by them publicly, has been the idea that an
acceleration in growth was being held back due to delayed reforms.
In the rest of this essay I discuss two issues pertaining to the idea
of inclusive growth, namely, how best it can be understood so
that economic policy can directly address it and whether we may
reasonably expect that high growth per se will deliver it within an
acceptable timeframe.

[1] Excerpt from Manmohan Singh's response to the No Confidence Motion,
Lok Sabha, 22 July 2008. See Singh (2008).

[2] Quoted in C. Rajamohan, 'If poverty has to go, growth must touch 10 per
cent and continue: FM', *The Indian Express*, 27 March 2008. Note the distinctly
welfarist tone.

Strategic factors in inclusive growth

To assess the prospects for inclusive growth in India today we need an understanding of what it entails. Two criteria are proposed here. First, for growth to be considered inclusive it must carry with it the largest numbers. With a view to concreteness, we may reduce this to the criterion of employment. For, though individuals benefit in various ways from faster growth, in an economy such as India's where welfare is yet to be institutionalized, gaining employment is the surest way to be included in a growing economy. Note that the criterion proposed here is extremely mild. We could, for instance, have adopted 'maximin' as our criterion, which would imply that growth is inclusive only when it maximizes the income of the worst off. A reasonable second criterion for inclusiveness would be that growth should cater to a wide range of our material needs, implying that growth must be spread across the various sectors of the economy. From such a perspective, we would be sceptical of high growth achieved, for instance, by turning the entire Indian economy into some kind of gigantic back-office to the rest of the world! Indeed, we are unlikely to find this edifying even if the export of software or information technology-enabled services (ITES) were to allow us to consume whatever we may need through imports. In any case, trade is unlikely to give us roads and parks or sewerage, all of which we would recognize as being important for the quality of our life. So all-round development of the economy emerges as an additional criterion for judging inclusiveness. This is not encountered much in the public debate on inclusiveness in India today, which is mainly confined to the first criterion proposed here, but upon reflection must come across as equally important. Taking on board these two criteria, we are better placed to identify the factors that are of strategic importance to achieving inclusive growth in this country.

The importance of agriculture and the role of education

We can see immediately that if there is dynamism in agriculture, it will come closest to satisfying both the criteria for inclusive growth proposed here at the same time. On the first count, as the largest share of the Indian workforce is rural, it is growth of this sector that, in the first instance, will carry along with it the largest possible number of workers. At the same time, going by the second criterion of inclusiveness, as India's households devote a large share of their budgets to food, progress in agriculture is essential if growth is to cater to the most pressing among our material needs. The performance of the agricultural sector since the onset of market liberalization in 1991 has, except in phases, been somewhat lacklustre. Specifically, the production of foodgrains has barely kept abreast of population growth. Though food requirements vary across the climatic zones of the globe, we get some perspective from a cross-country comparison. For Korea we find that the rate of growth of per capita production of food grew at an average annual rate of over 2 per cent per annum for three decades from the mid-1960s. This had, not surprisingly, been a period of exceptional dynamism for the Korean economy as a whole (see Hayami and Godo 2005). Interestingly, while the Indian government's official statements have often justified the reforms by reference to the East Asian experience, the agricultural quotient is mostly left out. With close to double-digit food-price inflation for three years running it is not too early to take a fresh look at the strategy that has been pursued in India since 1991.

So, we identify a dynamic agriculture as one pillar of our strategy for inclusive growth. However, acquiring this dynamism will require some non-trivial interventions. Faster agricultural growth requires an educational preparedness. Improved agricultural productivity today requires an educated farmer for dealing with the opportunities and threats that liberalization has brought to the sector and be able to face the greater ecological adversity due to creeping climate change. Secondly, in order to reduce the overcrowding that leads to the shrinking of farm sizes, a shifting of labour from that sector to the rest of the economy is needed. Actually, these potential non-agricultural workers will not only have to be educationally prepared but also professionally trained. Other instances can be imagined too. Suppose the liberalization pursued thus far were to generate greater opportunities for export of goods. To the extent that the production of goods for export requires a more educated workforce, the uneducated cannot take advantage of the opportunities that may be presented.[3] Greater integration with the world economy, which was a goal of the reforms initiated in 1991, will not necessarily contribute to inclusive growth even if it were to ensure an accelerated one. This leads us to the recognition of education as a necessary component of a strategy for inclusive growth.

Thus, attaining the goal of inclusive growth, viewed from diverse angles, requires a concerted effort to raise the level of educational preparedness of the Indian population. Given the education deficit in the country and the extreme inequality in its distribution across the population, the excessive focus of 'UPA II' on the very limited number of new Indian institutes of technology and of management may amount to no more than a matter of toying with the tip of the iceberg.[4] Hence, this may well be the moment to grasp the opportunity hitherto missed of both improving schooling and extending vocational training in the country. Empirical work on the role of education in India is relatively scarce. However, evidence of a better educated and socially developed west and south of the country growing faster than the rest is surely indicative of the centrality of education to both growth and development.

---

[3] A tension implied in the dichotomous 'economic development and social opportunity', the title of an early study of the reach of the original reform programme in India by Dreze and Sen (1995).

[4] For a historian's perspective on why higher education has systematically been privileged in India, we may turn to Thapar's (2009) account: '(M)any of us feel that the foundation of primary and secondary schools has still to be established and nurtured. I suspect that nothing is done about the foundation because political parties fear an educated electorate that can ask questions. It would then not be swayed by mass meetings and would make vote-banks irrelevant. The moment people ask questions and relate the present to the past and have a project for the future, it becomes a different electorate. I don't think it is just an oversight that governments and politicians pay so little attention to (basic) education.' This must count as an important instance in India's history of politics trumping economics.

The question of the market

The true significance of a market economy is not so much that there is little or no government intervention as much as that the level of production, and therefore, of employment is determined by the level of aggregate demand. The latter constitutes 'the market' for the economy's goods. For every national economy, there are two sources of demand—domestic and external. It appears that as India is among the poorest economies of the world, the rest of the world is a market readily available. References to the East Asian economies having made use of the global market to grow abound in the literature. Something close to this possibility appears to have been the premise underlying the reforms of 1991 that integrated India with the world economy, that is, a growth through trade would be initiated. While the opening up of the economy may have contributed somewhat to the growth of exports, as we can see by now, this has been far from sufficient to make a dent on unemployment in the country. This has to do with the fact that since the mid-1990s, software products and services and ITES have come to account for a large part of India's exports. These exports rely on skilled labour. On the other hand, manufactures mostly rely on less-skilled manual labour. However, as far as the prospects for exports from this sector are concerned, India faces strong competition from China. So the mere fact of a large supply of manual labour cannot assure India of automatic success upon opening up to trade. Poor educational levels and low vocational training of its labour are as much a constraint in raising manufactured exports as is the inadequacy of supporting infrastructure such as power, roads and ports.

The question of the market, as in the source of demand, has not been adequately faced in the official exercise of setting high growth targets for India. Once again, it was simply assumed that the opening up of the economy via trade liberalization would leave the global market for her taking. At the same time, the potential of the domestic economy as a market for its goods appears to have been ignored, though perhaps more by default rather than by design. A fundamental distinction between the domestic and foreign economies as markets is that a country has, via its national government, some control over determining the former but none whatsoever over the latter. The near instantaneous collapse of India's exports following the global slowing of 2007–08 points to this quite conclusively.[5] It reveals the limits of the strategy of relying solely on the world market for sustained growth. Clearly, at this stage of our economic development the objective should be to grow the domestic market while at the same doing everything necessary to benefit from access to the foreign one. In such a scenario, the role of trade reforms is relatively limited and a policy of releasing constraints on domestic production assert a priority. This need can hardly be viewed as a particularly radical solution. Since the global financial crisis, it is actually a solution that is recommended even by multilateral financial agencies.[6]

What is of significance here is the existence of a link between the internal market and inclusive growth. From this point of view, currently at least for India, it is the growth in agriculture that is likely to best serve the cause of a growing home market. With the largest share of the labour force concentrated in this sector, a rupee's worth of income earned in agriculture is spread over a larger number of workers than a rupee's worth of growth elsewhere in the economy and, at the current per capita income, more likely to be spent on goods produced by the relatively low-skilled labour concentrated in the non-agricultural sector. This mechanism boosts both demand and employment in the latter. The experience of Indian manufacturing in 2008–09 when the global slowing

---

[5] As an indication, note that by October 2009, exports had declined on a month-to-month basis for 13 consecutive months. The magnitudes are significant too. Over the first six months of 2009–10, the decline in exports was of the order of 26 per cent compared to the same period of the previous year (see 'Exports Continue to Decline in October', *The Hindu*, Kochi Edition, 2 December 2009). By 2014, export growth may have revived even as the growth rate has sagged, as if in illustration of the point that exports alone cannot be expected to prop up growth in India. For the most recent information on export growth see 'CAD narrows', *The Hindustan Times*, New Delhi, 6 March 2014.

[6] See Yunwei (2009) for the report: 'The Asian Development Bank said in an August report that the emerging nations need to value the expansion of domestic demand in order to realize their economy's balanced development.'

impacted it proportionately less than the slowdown in exports due to the unexpected cushion provided by public spending under the National Rural Employment Guarantee Act (NREGA), is a case in point. Note that NREG scheme is a limited scheme for employment generation in that it presently entitles one person in every family to 100 days of manual labour in one year. By comparison, faster agricultural growth may be expected to spread incomes much more widely among rural households, with implications for the growth of the internal market for manufactured goods. Thus, agricultural expansion led by productivity growth, especially in the production of food, is particularly conducive to inclusive growth. Since the first round of such an expansion would be rural-based, the largest number of households in the country benefit due to rising incomes. In the second round, this raises the demand for manufactures from these households. The significance of a productivity-led agricultural expansion, especially in the production of food, is that it makes a declining relative price of food compatible with growing farm profitability, a condition for sustained expansion of the agricultural sector. A declining relative price of food leaves urban households with greater purchasing power over manufactures. This is likely to lead to a secondary expansion in demand for products of the manufacturing sector, the first having come from rising incomes in the agricultural sector. This has been the economic history of most of the high income countries in the world, except perhaps of the oil-rich kingdoms in the Middle East. This is not a route that India has explored seriously or pursued in a sustained manner. Growth by expansion of the domestic market assumes relevance not only at a time when the effects of the financial meltdown are all too evident but also in the foreseeable future, when the Organisation for Economic Co-operation and Development (OECD) economies are likely to grow very slowly due to slowing demand attributable to an aging population growing gradually. These developments imply a slow-growing external market for Indian goods.[7] However, prospects of a declining relative price of

---

[7] There is though the promise of Africa where growth has accelerated every decade over the past five. See http://vc4africa.biz/blog/2011/10/13/three-reasons-to-take-a-new-look-at-investing-in-africa/; accessed on 6 January 2014.

food from rising agricultural productivity, a central element in this strategy, will require a departure from the current practice of the Indian government. For over three decades, it has been evident that governments are loath to allow a decline in agriculture's terms of trade irrespective of the profitability of farm production and have intervened in the grain markets accordingly. This is incompatible with the type of agriculture-led expansion of the wider economy that has been proposed here. That will require a far more flexible form of government intervention in the grain markets than has been the practice for a long time in India. Once again, politics impinges directly on economic possibilities here.

We have argued that a growth strategy that creates a domestic market for mass consumption goods is likely to be more inclusive, as the employment generated will be of the less-skilled workers. Two points about this strategy may be noted. First, even if it is geared towards absorption of less-skilled labour, the requirement of generally upgrading education and training in India cannot be escaped. Current levels of human resource development in India are low, and there are few signs of a hasty rectification of the situation. UNESCO's 'EFA Development Index' meant to capture a country's progress towards the goal of 'education for all' (EFA) by 2015 indicates very slow progress in India, which is ranked 105th out of 129 countries on this score (UNESCO 2007). Secondly, a strategy of growth via an expanding domestic market need not in any way imply neglecting opportunities offered by the foreign market. Effective participation in the two markets can be complementary. A large domestic market affords a size of operation that enables the exploitation of potential economies of scale, which will help Indian firms to compete in the global market. Historically, from Britain to Germany, the original exporters of manufactures have been great manufacturing nations to start with. This is not surprising. On account of the importance of static and dynamic economies of scale, a country with a large home market acquires an advantage over others when it comes to exports. Note that here the causation is seen as running from the efficiency of domestic production to external competitiveness. The same holds for upgradation of skills of the labour force. Even when intended to enable an expansion of production in response to domestic demand, competing on the global market is aided by a better human resource base. Once again, we would find that historically the great exporters of the world coming from distinct geographies and cultures have also had the most educated and skilled workers to start with.[8] In the absence of a well-trained workforce, an open trade regime per se is not much use from the point of view of growth through exports.[9]

The political barrier to attaining inclusive growth

So what stands in the way of adopting a growth strategy such as the one outlined here? First and foremost, there appears to be a failure to appreciate its relevance. For instance, while the Approach Paper to the XIth Plan does speak of the need for both inclusion and higher agricultural growth, it failed to identify the link between the two. The general premise appears to be that a higher growth rate is needed for inclusiveness to be attained, and faster agricultural growth is seen as the route to achieving higher economy-wide growth. As for the reforms of 1991, their adoption was influenced by the historical moment in which they were launched. The end of East-European communism had led to the unthinking rejection of any government intervention in the growth process, the market outcome being assumed to be optimal and therefore, best left not tampered with. So, the main task for India, it was interpreted, was to unleash competition within the economy while at the same time integrating it with the rest of the world. After close to two decades

[8] See Kim (1995) on how the creation of an educated labour force preceded industrialization in Korea.

[9] In work done for the World Bank in the 1980s, when the East Asian tigers had first caught the imagination of economists, Wheeler explicitly considered the question whether education and health matter 'beyond extraversion' or openness to trade. His econometric investigation yielded evidence of this, leading him to conclude that countries that ignore the development of their human resource 'will experience more difficulty in export expansion, with its attendant benefits, than their counterparts which have focused on human resources,' Wheeler (1984: 34).

of this, we can by now see that while liberalization of the policy regime was needed, was timely and has borne fruit, it does not constitute a growth strategy, leave alone guarantee inclusion. On the other hand, an agricultural expansion is constitutive of such a strategy and, as demonstrated earlier, stands a better chance of carrying along with it the largest numbers. A belated recognition of its importance appears to have been instigated by the outcome of the general elections in 2009. The result it seems has been interpreted as a case of rural voters rewarding the incumbent UPA government for paying attention to their welfare. However, this overlooks the fact that though the NREG scheme was in place, GDP in the agricultural sector had grown by a whopping 4.7 per cent in 2007–08, and this itself had followed two years of very high growth (see Economic Survey 2008–09) of the sector. An additional factor driving the interpretation that it was welfarism that was being rewarded by the electorate may have been that globally, the allure of the 'American Business Model' (see Kay 2003), privileging the claims of the corporate sector, had dimmed after the financial meltdown that originated in the United States. The meltdown revealed the claims for the Model's efficacy as bankrupt and the governments that had championed it as seriously culpable. As India is a democracy, the lesson could not but have been learned by its political class who now quickly moved to a welfarist mode. Nevertheless, very likely it was high rural growth rather than the welfare-oriented NREG scheme that buoyed the fortunes of the incumbent government. This takes us to the second factor that stands in the way of the success of the strategy for inclusive growth sketched here.

While a productivity-driven agricultural expansion supported by rising educational levels needs to be supported with resources, resources are unlikely to prove to be the binding constraint in attaining it. The tax–GDP ratio for India has distinctly risen since 2004–05 (see Economic Survey 2008–09). Anyway, some rationalization of expenditure on subsidies should yield finances for greater investment. However, even without the financial leeway this allows, a comparison of expenditure and outcome in the irrigation sector over the last decade clearly indicates that the government's finances may amount to less of a lacking than a proper use being made of them (see Balakrishnan et al. 2008). In another instance, public spending per student in elementary schooling increased by 50 per cent in the decade since 1993–94.[10] However, the findings of the only record of learning in India's schools available to us, namely the Annual Status of Education Report by the NGO Pratham, shows that poor learning outcomes continue in the primary school system. A third example of public spending not having the desired impact comes from the area of public nutrition programmes. International health researchers have found that the outcomes associated with the government's Integrated Child Development Services (ICDS) are poor. They track these outcomes back to poor governance of ICDS, a reasoning contained in their observation that poor nutrition in India co-exists with high economic growth (see Haddad 2009). A general message from these examples is that while in most areas of the economy where the government intervenes resources may no longer be the binding constraint, the capacity for effective governance very likely is. So long as a lack of accountability pervades the functioning of the government machinery, outcomes from more spending are likely to remain disappointing. Dreze and Sen (2013) point out that India's political class is united in a reluctance to enforce accountability within the public sector.

If it is considered obligatory to provide a ranking of the areas where intervention is necessary to make growth more inclusive in the long run than it has been so far, the following order suggests itself. It is governance, education and agriculture, in descending order of importance. As pointed out, with the largest number of Indians yet engaged in agriculture, any plan for making growth inclusive must start here. We have seen that faster agricultural growth requires better educational preparedness. This is also needed to enable the movement of labour from agriculture into manufacturing and services. While India has historically spent less

---

[10] See Mishra (2009); source cited 'Annual Financial Statistics of Education Sector 2003–04', MHRD, 2005. I am grateful to the author for permission to cite his findings.

on education than other countries in an international comparison, it is also clear that her public education system functions very poorly. Though he may have had the economy in mind, Prime Minister Manmohan Singh's observation about the economy being 'over regulated and under governed' (see Singh 2004) appears to be particularly true of this sector. Effective governance assumes a priority in the quest for inclusive growth.

We have attempted to reduce to their most basic the elements that go into an inclusive growth process. The result may appear as offering a nicely ordered set of interventions. However, the world is much more complex than what may have been implicitly assumed here and, therefore, what has been proposed is not the only plausible ordering. In reality, a more prosperous agriculture, however attained, may encourage the private adoption of higher educational goals, and a better educated populace will be a force for more democratic governance. Now we have the sequence reversed! Nevertheless, in the event of a willing and capable government, or one that is goaded in this direction, the sequence of interventions starting with improved governance constitutes a feasible growth strategy. Moreover, it is likely to achieve quicker results than allowing for the alternative scenario sketched earlier to work itself out. It may reasonably be expected that following the success of the Aam Aadmi Party, the other political parties have internalized the message that the electorate expects a government that functions and that providing one is crucial for their returning to power.

We have outlined a strategy that is more likely than others to generate growth with inclusion at this juncture. Going by this, we can say that while an agriculture-driven growth process supported by the necessary educational interventions can yield a higher growth rate while carrying the largest possible numbers with it, a high growth rate per se, when attained by other means, need not necessarily be inclusive. We are able to state this with some confidence as there is the recent Indian experience to go by. Indeed, it is the fact of the very high growth over 2003–08 not being satisfactory on this count that had led to inclusion being placed on the political agenda in the first instance. While the architects of India's reforms may well be motivated by a desire to see an inclusive economy, their pronouncements—some of which have been reproduced here—indicate that they privilege high growth over other instruments as a means of bringing it about.[11] This perspective may be contrasted with the view advanced by us that, at least within a range, the composition of growth may matter more for inclusion and that much can be achieved without additional resources so long as governance improves. On the other hand, mere injection of funds without improved governance could conceivably end up delivering neither higher growth nor inclusiveness.

Conclusion

The central challenge in attaining inclusive growth is empowering the poor economically. While welfare transfers are a necessary form of income support for the poor, they do not constitute economic empowerment. The strategy proposed in this essay is addressed to the question of what is necessary for the poorest to earn permanently higher incomes. And the needed interventions have been specified. Essentially, for the poor to be lifted out of poverty, they need to be turned into producers. This requires both that they be equipped for the task and a market be created for what they produce. The challenge for policy is to engineer this joint outcome. It is clear that to successfully bring about inclusive growth in India today, economic policy needs to be more focused on the domestic economy than it has been in the past two decades. Over this period, the attention has largely been on the interface between India and the rest of the world. While this site must continue to receive our fullest attention, it is of limited value when it comes to designing a programme for inclusion. Our analysis has reduced the elements that go into inclusive growth to effective governance, as educationally equipping the poor to be producers and ensuring a market for the goods that they produce, initially via accelerated agricultural growth, is today constrained more by

[11] See the statements by Manmohan Singh and P. Chidambaram reproduced earlier on.

governance than it is by resources. Arguably, in the immediate future, prospects for inclusive growth in the Indian economy turn on reform of the institutions of government so that the best use is made of the (wo)men and materials harnessed using public funds. Exhortation that the economic reforms launched in 1991 should continue must henceforth be diverted to address this aspect rather than the mere liberalization of the policy regime—the project has in any case travelled some distance by now. As governance is ultimately a political outcome, it is politics that will determine the possibility of inclusive growth in India.

References

Balakrishnan, P., R. Golait and P. Kumar. (2008). 'Agricultural Growth in India since 1991', DRG Paper No. 27, Mumbai: Reserve Bank of India.

Dreze, J. and A. Sen. (1995). *Economic Development and Social Opportunity*. New Delhi: Oxford University Press.

Dreze, J. and A. Sen. (2013). *Uncertain Glory: India and its Contradictions*. Princeton: Princeton University Press.

Haddad, L. (2009). 'Economic powerhouse or nutritional weakling?', *The Hindu*, Kochi edition, 15 September.

Hayami, Y. and Y. Godo. (2005). *Development Economics: From the Poverty to the Wealth of Nations*, Third Edition. New York: Oxford University Press.

Kay, J. (2003). *The Truth About Markets*. London: Penguin Books.

Kim, L. (1995). 'Absorptive capacity and industrial growth: A conceptual framework and Korea's Experience', in B.H. Koo and D.H. Perkins (eds), *Social capability and long-term economic growth*. New York: St. Martin's Press.

Mishra, A.D. (2009) 'Financing of higher education: a shifting pattern', paper presented at the Fifth Young Scholars' Programme, Mumbai: UNDP and IGIDR, mimeo, National University of Educational Planning and Administration, New Delhi.

Planning Commission. (2006). *Towards Faster and More Inclusive Growth: An Approach to the 11th Five-Year Plan*. New Delhi: Planning Commission.

Singh, M. (2004). 'Prime Minister's Address', All-India Conference of Lokayuktas and Uplokayuktas at Dehradun, 29 September. Press Release of the Government of India. Available at: http://pib.nic.in/release.

Singh, M. (2008). 'Prime Minister's reply to the debate on the Motion of Confidence in the Lok Sabha', 22 July. Available at: http://pmindia.nic.in/speeches.htm.

Thapar, R. (2009). 'Conversations about history, An interview with Kalpana Sharma', *The Hindu*, 25 January.

Wheeler, D. (1984). *Human Resource Policies, Economic Growth, and Demographic Change in Developing Countries*. Oxford: The Clarendon Press.

Yunwei, F. (2009). 'Emerging economies strive for development amid challenges', *The Hindu*, Kochi, 16 September.

POLICY

Chapter 9

Informality: Mindsets and Policies

*Ravi Kanbur**

Introduction

The informal economy comprises those economic activities which are beyond the purview of the state because they lie outside its framework of laws, regulations and protections. A small proportion of these activities are illegal, but mostly they are activities which are not covered by the state's rules and regulations. The informal economy is of great concern for policymakers the world over, and Indian policymakers are no exception. The core economic reasons for this concern are the strong association of informality with poverty and with low productivity. But the roots of the recent preoccupation with informality lie in the tension between two opposing forces. One of these is a historical policy mindset built on the expectation that informality will decline and disappear with development. The other is a global trend which shows that

* This essay is an expansion and adaptation of a presentation to the Economic Development Department of the Presidency of the Republic of South Africa (20 February 2013).

informality is not declining as fast as might be expected with economic growth, and indeed in some cases, not declining at all but increasing.

This essay's objective is complementing the 'politics trumps economics' theme of this volume by exploring how mindsets influence policymaking and how they tend to persist even in the face of counter trends in reality. I first develop the history of economic thought and policymaking on informality so as to establish the route through which we came to be where we are today. I then present the main global trends on informality and discuss some possible explanations for them. In light of this discussion, I then turn to policy and most importantly, how to change the mindsets of those who formulate and implement the policy on informality.

Frameworks and mindsets

There are two main historical sources of the current policy mindset on informality—academic and administrative. But these two strands are interwoven with each other. The early academic and analytical literature on development economics is dominated by 'dual economy' models, where the dualism is modelled as being between a 'modern' (or capitalist, or industrial, or urban, or formal) sector and a 'traditional' (household enterprise, or agricultural, or rural, or informal) sector. The modern sector is the one which is governed by the laws of the state.

The details vary, but a central proposition, for example in the famous Lewis 'surplus labour' model of development, is the tendency for the modern sector to grow relative to the traditional sector during the process of development (Lewis 1954). Empirical support for this is often provided by ranking a cross-section of countries by their per capita incomes and noting that measures of industrialization, urbanization, formalization, and so on, increase with income. These models and these snapshot stylized facts across countries are so ingrained in our thinking that measures, such as of industrialization, or urbanization, or informality are sometimes used as measures of development itself. The mindset is thus that informality should decline into insignificance as development takes place and as per capita incomes rise.

A different but related part of academic literature is represented by the strand which owes its beginning to the classic paper by Harris and Todaro (1970). In this perspective, the economy is once again divided into two sectors, a formal sector which is affected by a range of government regulations, and an informal sector which is not. In the specific context of the labour market, for example, the formal sector has a government-enforced minimum wage which is set above the competitive level. This reduces labour demand in the formal sector, with the excess supply of labour moving to the informal sector, which does not have any labour market regulations. Competition clears the informal labour market at a lower wage. Thus, the informal sector represents the ideal of a competitive labour market, while the formal sector labour market is 'distorted' by government interventions. The policy stance emerging from this perspective focuses on de-regulation in the formal sector in order to reduce the size of the informal economy.

As a final example of the academic mindset in relation to informality, consider the line of argument attributed to Hernando de Soto (2003), reflected, for example, in the report of the United Nations High Level Commission on Legal Empowerment of the Poor (United Nations 2008). Here the main issue is highlighted as the lack of formal legal frameworks in the informal economy—indeed, informality is defined as the lack of such frameworks. The policy conclusion is an attempt to make the informal into the formal by extending the reach of formal structures into areas such as urban slums. A major criticism is that such attempts simply try to translate or implant formal structures into an informal setting without a full understanding of the repercussions (Basu et al. 2011).

The administrative mindset on informality has somewhat more complex roots. It is best illustrated by a strand of dual economy literature which goes back to colonial times. The term 'dual economy' was coined by the Dutch anthropologist and colonial administrator J.H. Boeke in his characterization of the economy of the Dutch East Indies (Boeke 1953). The distinction here was between those activities that fell under the purview of colonial rules and regulations, and those activities that were beyond the legal and administrative reach of the colonial government. My reading of colonial administrative literature brings to mind the notion of a wall which separates the formal from the informal (see Basu et al. 2011; Ghani and Kanbur 2012). On this side of the wall is the well-ordered colonial state, subject to a set of laws and regulations, managed by its administrators and officials. On that side of the wall is the (mostly native) informal economy, ill understood and misunderstood by colonial policymakers. It is perceived to be chaotic, disorganized, and possibly with criminal elements.

The colonial yoke has been lifted but not the mindset. Postcolonial administrators the world over, particularly at the local level, appear to have the same mindset as their colonial predecessors. Informality is a symbol of underdevelopment, a nuisance to be swept away and kept out of sight in the modernizing path of the national economy (Guha-Khasnobis et al. 2006). This meshes conveniently with the academic mindset which sees informality in any case dwindling with development.

Levels and trends

The second set of points I wish to make relate to the basic global facts of informality. This requires us to first delve a little into the somewhat technical matter of measuring informality. While the measurement of urbanization, or of industrialization, is not without its difficulties, these pale into insignificance compared with the issues raised by a measurement of informality.

Starting with the basic conceptualization that an informal economic activity is that which is outside the framework of the state's laws, regulations and protections, the question is how do we translate this into a measurable entity to which the national machinery of statistical measurement can be applied? This requires us to specify the particular laws and regulations relative to which formality or informality is to be identified. One route is through economic enterprises, and applying the filter of those enterprises which are private unincorporated enterprises, 'that is, enterprises owned by individuals or households that are not constituted as separate legal entities independent of their owners' (ILO 1993: paragraph 5). But the definition of incorporation can vary from country to country, and often the measurements available turn out to be a function of the laws in place.

A case in point is the distinction between the 'organized' and the 'unorganized' sectors in Indian manufacturing. This distinction is often used interchangeably with the distinction between 'formality' and 'informality' in the Indian context. India's Factories Act of 1948 requires all manufacturing enterprises with 10 or more workers (20 or more workers if the enterprise does not use electricity) to register with the authorities and to implement certain health, safety and other regulations. The registration then provides a count of such enterprises and can be used as a measure of the size of the 'organized' (or formal) sector in manufacturing.

However, such clean-cut definitions, emerging out of the rules and regulations themselves, are not necessarily available in many or even in most countries. In addition, there are criticisms of such an enterprise-based perspective. An alternative, worker-based perspective is to ask if a worker has or does not have employer provided security of different types. Recent approaches to informality have adopted this broader definition. For example, India's National Commission on Employment in the Unorganized Sector (NCEUS) states the broadening as:

> The informal sector consists of all unincorporated private enterprises owned by individuals or households engaged in the sale and production of goods and services operated on a proprietary or partnership basis and with less than ten total workers… Informal workers consist of those working in the informal sector or households, excluding regular workers with social security benefits by the employers, and the workers in the formal sector without any employment and social security benefits provided by the employers (NCEUS 2008: 2).

These conceptual and statistical intricacies of defining and measuring informality have led to a large academic and technical literature. This is not the occasion to go deeper into these issues. Especially when it comes to cross-country comparisons and trends, a number of compromises have to be made in order to develop data series (Charmes 2012: 114).

What, then, is known about global patterns of informality? The rate of informality, as measured by the fraction of the total labour force employed in the informal economy, varies greatly across the world. Latin American rates are relatively low, in the 40–50 per cent range, while African rates are higher, in the 60–70 per cent range. South Africa is known to be an anomaly in Africa with rates in the 20–30 per cent range, depending on the exact measure used. South Asia has the highest rates of informality in the world. India, for example, has rates in the 80–90 per cent range (Jutting and de Laglesia 2009; Ghani and Kanbur 2012).

What about trends in informality? A recent comprehensive study by Charmes (2012), presents the following summary:

In average for the [North Africa] region, the most recent period is characterised by a huge increase of employment in the informal economy, growing from 47.3% at the beginning of the 2000s up to 58.1% at the end of the decade.... For sub-Saharan Africa...the figures for the region give an image of a continuously growing informal economy (from more than 60% in the 1970s and mid-1980s, to more than 70% at the end of the 1980s-beginning of the 1990s and more than 80% at the end of the 1990s), until the years 2000s, which seem to be characterised by a decrease.... In Latin America, employment in the informal economy seems on the rise, increasing from 54.2% at the end of the 1990s up to 57.7% at the end of the years 2000s.... In Southern and South-Eastern Asia, employment in the informal economy is stabilised around 70% of non-agricultural employment...ranging from 41.1% in Thailand to 84.2% in India and 86.4% in Nepal.... Lastly, transition countries are making their way out of their former administered-centralised-wage economies and they see their share of employment in the informal economy... increasing little by little from 20.7% at the beginning of the years 2000s, up to 27% at the end of the decade.

Thus, the global picture is mixed, with some regional variations, but overall, it would be fair to say that there is not a strong tendency for informality to decline, as would be predicted by the academic textbooks and as expected by policy administrators. Country-specific work for India largely confirms the sluggish decline, if not an actual increase, in informality despite dramatically higher growth rates compared to historical experience (Ghani and Kanbur 2012; Jutting and de Laglesia 2009).

What explains this persistence of informality in the face of economic growth in the last quarter century? There are two main explanations which are debated by analysts. The first is 'regulation'. It is argued that informality is caused by excessive regulation in the formal sector, which creates incentives for economic activity to operate outside the purview of regulations—informality, in other words. But even if the presence of regulation could explain the *level* of informality, for it to explain *increases* in informality the regulatory burden would have had to have *increased*. But, in fact, it is well appreciated that in the last two decades of liberalization, the regulatory burden has if anything *decreased*. The regulation-based explanation of increasing informality is thus weak at best.

The second main explanation has to do with fundamental trends in technology and trade which have reduced the employment intensity of growth in the formal sector. The 'jobless growth' phenomenon means that the formal sector cannot provide employment for a growing labour force, which then has to go into either open unemployment or the informal sector. The technology/ trade explanation seems to me to be a more plausible one for trends in informality. But if one accepts this then since the forces shaping technology and trade are unlikely to reverse in the next two decades, we are also forced to accept that informality is here to stay. Far from receding as a result of development, the very nature of current development means that it will increase. A recent OECD report asked the question in its title: 'Is Informal Normal?' The answer it gave was a definite 'Yes' (Jutting and de Laglesia 2009).

Tensions and responses

When the irresistible force of increasing informality meets the immovable object of current academic and administrative mindsets, tensions arise which are reflected in policy schizophrenia. Different parts of the government end up doing different, contradictory, interventions. Sometimes, even the same part of the government gives with one hand and takes away with the other. The result is that the government as a whole shows policy incoherence, and ends up giving mixed signals.

These are phenomena we see around the world. In India, for example, the government has introduced a plethora of schemes to support workers in the informal economy, including training schemes and support for savings and investments by small operators. However, at the same time, urban administrators have become enamoured of the 'city of the future' label, with a mindset which sees the informal sector as something of a nuisance in achieving this goal. For instance, the city of Ahmedabad has designated some of its new roads 'modern', along which no street vending is to be allowed. Cities and governments are also vying to stage international events—the Commonwealth Games in the case of India's capital, Delhi. The new stadiums and the flyovers lead to huge displacement of informal activities, with inadequate and inappropriate allocation of new space for these activities. In the rush to become what they think Singapore looks like, cities in the developing world are trying to sweep away the informal economy. But the global trends identified in the previous section suggest that this will ultimately be unsuccessful. Indeed, recent research seems to suggest that urbanization goes hand in hand with informalization (Ghani and Kanbur 2012).

There is a plethora of technical issues which can be related to the design of policy to address the needs of the informal economy. Examples include the extension of financial services, the development of skills through training programmes, better infrastructure for small-scale enterprises and so on. However, in my view, a central problem in addressing informality goes back to the policy mindset, which on the one hand views the phenomenon as being 'on the other side of the wall' and on the other hand as being 'on the way out' since formalization is expected to increase during the process of growth and development. But the informal economy is here to stay, at least for quite a while, and as the name suggests, it is indeed part of the overall economy. Its success and development is essential for overall economic development and for poverty reduction.

Policymakers and policy implementers are, of course, part of the formal economy. Their own lives are governed by rules, laws and regulations which are framed by the state. Their economic life has a regularity and a stability guaranteed by the state. This is very different from life in the informal economy. This difference is captured very well by Keith Hart, the anthropologist credited with coining the term 'informality' in the 1970s, and with the early development of the concept, based on his work on the slums in Accra, the capital of Ghana in West Africa:

> The main message....was that Accra's poor were not 'unemployed.' They worked, often casually, for erratic and generally low returns; but they were definitely working... Following Weber, I argued that the ability to stabilize economic activity within a bureaucratic form made returns more calculable and regular for the workers as well as their bosses. That stability was in turn guaranteed by the state's laws, which only extended so far into the depths of Ghana's economy. 'Formal' incomes came from regulated economic activities, and 'informal' incomes, both legal and illegal, lay beyond the scope of regulation. I did not identify the informal economy with a place or a class or even whole persons. Everyone in Accra, but especially the inhabitants of the slum where I lived, tried to combine the two sources of income. Informal opportunities ranged from market gardening and brewing through every kind

of trade to gambling, theft, and political corruption (Hart 2006: 25).

The irregularities and uncertainties of the informal economy contrast sharply with the regularities and certainties of the economic lives of those who make and implement policies which affect them, and this disconnect is reflected often in policies and interventions. A good example, almost universal, is the ubiquitous requirement in the formal economy for establishing: (i) proof of identity and (ii) proof of residence for a whole host of economic interactions, particularly in the financial sphere. Proof of identity is required through documents like passports, driving licences and voter registration cards. Proof of residence is more problematic, requiring in some cases documents such as three consecutive utility bills with the name of the person on them. This is clearly not possible for those living in slums renting a room in a building from a landlord, and yet these are often the documents that are required.

Yet another example of the disconnect between the economic lives of policymakers and those for whom they make policy is provided by the thorny question of street vending and urban space. Loitering and vagrancy laws are often used by the police at the behest of local residents to clear away street vendors from public spaces. Street vendors are seen as dirtying clean spaces and obstructing living spaces in various urban neighbourhoods. But street vending is the principal livelihood for many in the informal economy. Thus, we see the almost daily drama of groups of informal traders being moved from one place, only to congregate in another and perhaps eventually cycling back to the same place when the attention of the police is elsewhere. In the process, an entire class of economic activity is criminalized.

The daily drama turns into a mega crisis when nations and cities host major international events, like the Commonwealth Games in Delhi, the World Cup in South Africa or the World Cup and the Olympics in Brazil. 'Beautification' programmes in preparation for an event that lasts a few weeks lead to the displacement of thousands of informal sector workers from their normal place of trading and work. A different but conceptually similar crisis occurs when the work of garbage pickers is displaced by formalized mechanisms with contracts given to big companies. The policy mindset is such as to always view this move favourably as being towards modernity and formality.

How can this mindset, which is deeply rooted in our academic and administrative roots, be changed? An enhanced technical analysis which highlights the true nature of the informal economy, its challenges and its contributions and the causes behind global trends in informality, will help of course. But changing the mindset will need more. In my view it will require removing, or at least reducing, the disconnect from the realities of the lives of policy analysts, policymakers and policy implementers on the one hand, and the lives in the informal economy on the other. I now turn to this issue.

The disconnect discussed earlier in the context of informality is part of a wider disconnect between the poor and those who analyse, formulate and implement policies on their behalf. As Robert Chambers (1995: 203–04) famously observed: '...it would seem that it is we the professionals, the powerful and the influential, and those who attend roundtables and summits, who have to reconstruct our reality, to change as people...'

I have written extensively about the nature of this disconnect (Kanbur 2011, 2012; Bali et al. 2012), with a particular focus on what to do about it. The key element, I have argued, is providing an insight into the 'live realities of the lives that will be affected by policy, through what are known as "immersions" or "exposure and dialogue programmes" (EDPs).' Eyben (2004: 2) characterizes these as exercises:

> ...designed for visitors to stay for a period of several days, living with their hosts as participants, as well as observers, in their daily lives. They are distinct from project monitoring or highly structured 'red carpet' trips when officials make brief visits to a village or an urban slum....

An account of such exercises carried out by a group of academics, activists and policymakers is provided in Bali et al. (2012).

The academics were economic analysts mainly from Cornell University. The process, of which I was a part, involved this group spending a few days and nights living and working with those who make their living from the informal economy. The EDP was conducted in India (twice), South Africa (twice) and Mexico (once), facilitated by local civil society organizations who worked with workers in the informal economy. In India we worked with the Self Employed Women's Association (SEWA). After being exposed to the lives and working conditions of our host ladies from SEWA, there was a period of dialogue where conventional technical and policy issues were discussed, but this time framed by the lived experience of the informal economy itself. These discussions are published in Bali et al. (2012).

The impact of the EDP on the outside participants was immense. As an independent evaluation of the process noted:

> Without exception, the Cornell economists all said that their time in the host households and their discussions with informal workers about their lives had given them a deeper understanding and had led to many new questions for debate in the subsequent dialogues and for later analytical work.... One economist, from a developing country, who felt he knew his own country well and was therefore sceptical about whether the EDP would provide him with anything new, said: 'I now truly believe that there is so much that researchers can get out of these interactions, and it breaks down the hierarchies that we all operate with' (Addison 2012: 630).

Reports of such 'immersion' exercises carried out by a number of agencies invariably point to the sensitization of outside participants to ground-level realities of life in the informal economy in a way that makes it unforgettable and leaves an indelible mark on future analysis and interventions. A special issue of the journal *Participatory Learning and Action* (2007) is devoted to the topic and records the experiences of a wide range of agencies.

A number of international development agencies, including the World Bank, have experimented with such immersion exercises. What is interesting, and perhaps surprising, is that they have not really been tried by governments in developing countries for their officials. My personal experience, when I suggest the exercise in different settings, is that the greatest resistance does indeed come from developing country officials. These responses echo those which Ruparel (2007: 39 –40) refers to in the context of the NGO Action Aid:

The usual reason for not participating is: 'I don't have the time.' This usually means: 'I can't, or won't, make this my priority for my time.' We manage to make time for workshops in capital cities and for training courses, but we find it difficult to make time to spend with poor people, building relationships with them, and really listening to the voices that we don't usually hear…. Another reason given for not doing immersions is: 'I come from a village, I don't need to do this.' While it is often the case that staff have such a background, an immersion offers an opportunity for them to stay with different communities that don't know them, their roles, and their status.

Resistance from officials, which is particularly marked in government ministries and agencies, is itself a reflection of the disconnect between the formal and the informal. EDPs, or immersions, are a tool for breaking through this disconnect in the interest of better informed formulation and implementation of policy. As I have argued elsewhere:

A central finding emerges from these and other experiences. Those who have experienced immersions are their greatest supporters. Those who have not are more likely to be sceptical. This scepticism has the potential to lead to a bad equilibrium where immersions are not done because they are not done. The only way this equilibrium can be broken is through outside action—for example, by a mandatory requirement from their management that all staff in all development agencies, whether official or non-governmental, undertake an immersion at least once in their career and preferably at key points in their career such as at appointment and promotion. Indeed, participation in an immersion in the current position could be made a basic qualification for promotion. I can of course see the objections to this, that it becomes yet another box-checking exercise on the career ladder. But we have such box-checking all over the place. For example, having taken certain courses, or attended certain seminars, are indeed often requirements for even being considered for promotion within these agencies. I can think of worse forms of box-checking than that staff in a development organization actually have spent a few nights living with those whose lives the organization seeks to improve (Kanbur 2012: 25).

Conclusion

I present the argument in this essay as a complement to the theme that 'politics trumps economics'. The argument might be summarized as 'mindset ignores trends', with negative consequences for the economy. Not forever, of course. Eventually, reality must make itself felt, the only question is how quickly, and how effectively we can respond. I have argued that a mindset that sees informality both as 'on the other side of the wall' and 'on the way out' is confronting the reality that the informal economy is not declining and is a normal part of the economy. Thus, the association of informality with poverty and low productivity needs to be confronted directly. However, attempts to do so, well intentioned though they might be, are impeded by the simple fact that policy analysts, policymakers and policy implementers are themselves part of the formal economy and thus tend to operate in that frame. The analyses conducted, the interventions proposed and their implementation, bear the hallmarks of that mindset. There is no simple answer to this conundrum, but I have made a particular proposal, based on the experience of EDPs and immersions. It is that analysts, policymakers and implementers should get some exposure to lives in the informal economy.

References

Addison, Tony. (2012). 'Bridging Different Perspectives on Labour and Poverty: An Evaluation', in Namrata Bali, Martha Chen and Ravi Kanbur (eds), *The Cornell-SEWA-WIEGO Exposure Dialogue Programme on Labor, Informal Employment and Poverty.* Ahmedabad: SEWA Academy, pp. 621–40.

Bali, Namrata, Martha Chen and Ravi Kanbur (eds). (2012). *Bridging Perspectives: The Cornell-SEWA-WIEGO Exposure Dialogue Programme on Labor, Informal Employment and Poverty.* Ahmedabad: SEWA Academy.

Boeke, Julius H. (1953). *Economics and Economic Policy of Dual Societies as Exemplified by Indonesia.* New York: Institute of Pacific Relations.

Basu, Arnab, Nancu Chau and Ravi Kanbur. (2011). 'Contractual Dualism, Market Power and Informality'. Available at: http://www.kanbur.dyson.cornell.edu/papers/BasuChauKanburContractualDualism.pdf.

Chambers, Robert. (1995). 'Poverty and Livelihoods: Whose Reality Counts?' *Environment and Urbanization*, 7 (1): 173–204.

Charmes, Jacques. (2012). 'The Informal Economy Worldwide: Trends and Characteristics', *Margin: The Journal of Applied Economic Research*, 6 (2): 103–32.

de Soto, Hernando. (2003). *The Mystery of Capital: Why Capitalism Triumphs in the West and Fails Everywhere Else.* New York: Basic Books.

Eyben, R. (2004). 'Immersions for policy and personal change', *IDS Policy Briefing*, 22. Brighton: Institute of Development Studies. Available at: www.ids.ac.uk/index.cfm?objectid=01D83AFF-5056-8171-7B4A44637F02E6E0.

Ghani, Ejaz and Ravi Kanbur. (2012). 'Urbanization and (In) Formalization'. Available at: http://kanbur.dyson.cornell.edu/papers/UrbanizationAndInformalization.pdf; accessed on 20 February 2013.

Guha-Khasnobis, Basudeb, Ravi Kanbur and Elinor Ostrom. (2006). 'Beyond Formality and Informality', in Basudeb Guha-Khasnobis, Ravi Kanbur and Elinor Ostrom (eds), *Linking the Formal and Informal Economy: Concepts and Policies*. Oxford: Oxford University Press, pp. 1–18.

Harris, John and Michael Todaro. (1970). 'Migration, Unemployment and Development: A Two Sector Analysis', *American Economic Review*, 60 (1): 126–42.

Hart, Keith. (2006). 'Bureaucratic Form and the Informal Economy', in Basudeb Guha-Khasnobis, Ravi Kanbur and Elinor Ostrom (eds), *Linking the Formal and Informal Economy: Concepts and Policies*. Oxford, UK: Oxford University Press, pp. 21–35.

International Labour Organization. (1993). *Resolutions Concerning Statistics of Employment in the Informal Sector Adopted by the 15th International Conference of Labour Statisticians*. Geneva: ILO.

Jutting, Johannes P. and Juan R. de Laglesia (eds). (2009). *Is Informal Normal? Towards More and Better Jobs In Developing Countries*. Paris: OECD.

Kanbur, Ravi. (2011). 'Poverty Professionals and Poverty', in A. Cornwall and I. Scoones (eds), *Revolutionizing Development*. London: Earthscan, pp. 211–16.

Kanbur, Ravi. (2012). 'Exposure and Dialogue Programs in the Training of Development Analysts and Practitioners'. Available at: http://www.kanbur.dyson.cornell.edu/papers/ExposureAndDialogue ProgramsTraining.pdf.

Lewis, W. Arthur. (1954). 'Economic Development with Unlimited Supplied of Labour', *Manchester School of Economic and Social Studies*, 22: 139–91.

National Commission on Employment in the Unorganized Sector. (2008). *The Challenge of Employment in India: An Informal Economy Perspective*. Available at: http://www.socialprotectionasia.org/ pdf/11.%20The_Challenge_of_Employment_in_India%20-%20 NCEUS%20-%20april%202009.pdf; accessed on 20 February 2013.

Ruparel, Sonya. (2007). 'Immersions in Action Aid', *Participatory Learning and Action*, 57: 36–40.

United Nations. (2008). *Making the Law Work for Everyone*. Report of the Commission on Legal Empowerment of the Poor. Available at: http://www.thepowerofthepoor.com/desoto/Making-the-Law-Work-for-Everyone.pdf.

Chapter 10

Innovation: The World's Most Generous Tax Regime

Sunil Mani

Introduction

The role played by technological improvements and innovation in spurring and maintaining high rates of economic growth is now fairly well understood. Recent economic histories of East Asian countries such as Korea and Taiwan have further provided empirical evidence for this belief. India, too, gave much importance to technological development right through the initial period when she started subscribing to a planned form of economic growth and development. One of the main objectives of the Five Year Plans was economic growth with technological self-reliance. Over the last three years, 2011–13, the Government of India has been on a policy spree. A number of policy documents ranging from those relating to specific industries such as automobiles, biotechnology, chemicals, electronics, electrical equipment, information technology and telecommunications to a more general policy on manufacturing and a science, technology and innovation policy have been published at a rather feverish pitch. It is almost as if the underlying belief is that having some policy statements is better than having no policy at all. Moreover, these policy exercises have had the positive effect of bringing in some strategic thinking with respect to very specific sectors. This sort of strategic thinking is necessary for an important area like innovation, where in a situation of fast-changing technologies and the catching up strategies successfully unfolded by many countries, especially in Asia, it is very essential for an emerging country like India to have a clearly articulated set of policy instruments and institutions to enable the country to achieve the kind of technological leadership that she is aspiring for. The most recent policy for promoting innovation is the Science, Technology and Innovation Policy of 2013. This exercise was preceded by a number of statements and quasi-policy documents on innovation such as the aborted attempt at passing a National Innovation Act, the rather long conversation in effecting an act which aimed at incentivizing publicly funded research (the Protection and Utilization of Public Funded Intellectual Property Bill, 2008).

Given the recent setback in India's macroeconomic performance with the slowing down of GDP growth, policy analysts have been quick to blame a sort of 'policy paralysis' which seems to have gripped the country's economic decision-making process. However, with a plethora of policy documents on every conceivable industry/ sector or issue, perhaps what we lack are not policies but their lackadaisical implementation. Most of the policy documents, especially at the sectoral level are stated in such general and vague terms that their actual implementation will be next to impossible or at best difficult to track over time. More importantly, most of these sectoral policy documents are virtually silent on whether the policy implementation will be subject to any form of concurrent evaluation. In fact, the lack of this important practice has virtually made the laudable objectives of earlier policies remaining just on paper even now.

As far as science and technology development is concerned, since independence India has had four policies for this, namely, the

Scientific Policy Resolution of 1958, the Statement on Technology Policy in 1983, the New Science and Technology Policy of 2003 and the Science, Technology and Innovation Policy of 2013. One can see from the titles of these policies that they proceeded from promoting science to science and technology to innovation. Further, there have been a number of specific policies dealing with specific institutions or instruments for promoting innovations such as the policy on patents or providing tax incentives for increasing the quantity of research and development (R&D). Then there are policies, which are targeted at specific sectors such as, for instance, the automotive or the information and communicatin technology (ICT) sectors. The former may be referred to as horizontal and the latter as vertical policies.

In an attempt at increasing innovations by domestic firms, India has been on a policy spree. For this the government has announced a series of policies both at the aggregate level and across specific sectors. This essay undertakes a survey of various policies and focuses its attention on one specific policy devised to subsidize R&D. Frequent elaboration of the R&D tax incentive scheme has made India a country with one of the most generous regimes for promoting in-house R&D by the corporate sector. An analysis of the outcomes shows that investment in R&D has actually been concentrated in a few industrial sectors and there is no evidence to show that the performance of firms with respect to R&D has actually improved. Policymaking with respect to promoting innovations has often got embroiled in political controversies of sorts. A good example of this is the government's attempt to develop telecommunications equipment technologies consistent with the usage pattern prevailing in the country. A public laboratory, the Centre for Development of Telematics (C-DOT) was set up in 1985. The laboratory was charged with the responsibility of developing a family of digital switching equipment that was consistent with the usage pattern prevailing in India within a short period of three years. The fact that the laboratory suffered a time over-run in executing this complex technology project was used as an excuse by the political bosses (in this case the minister for communications) and the bureaucracy to effectively wreck that fine experiment in technological self-reliance. Although, 'the C-DOT case'[1] is a specific one, it is by no means an isolated one. Similar examples can be found elsewhere as well where politics has managed to outrank or defeat economics. Wrecking domestic attempts at creating technologies primarily on political grounds has been a rather unpleasant feature of the process of technological development in the country.

In the context, the purpose of this essay is to first undertake a survey of horizontal and vertical policies. This is followed by an evaluation of one of the most direct policies for promoting innovation at the level of firms as firms are at the core of a country's National System of Innovation (NSI). The policy in question is the R&D tax policy that has been tried out by countries across the world as a way of encouraging firms to commit more resources to R&D. Over the years, India has elaborated on its R&D tax policy in such a manner that the country has the most generous R&D tax regime anywhere in the world. But has this led to significant increases in R&D investments by firms? This essay attempts to answer this question.

The rest of the essay is organized as follows. In the next section, we undertake a brief review of the major horizontal policies in as much as they incentivized technology development by business enterprises. The next section reviews the changes in the tax policy towards R&D as India now has one of the most generous R&D tax policies in the world. The last section provides a conclusion by assessing the impact of these policies on innovative activities by business enterprises.

Policies for promoting innovations by firms

Policies for increasing the generation and diffusion of innovations can broadly be categorized into two: horizontal and vertical. The

---

[1] More specific details of the politicization of the C-DOT experiment can be found in Mani (1995).

former deals with general policies, which lay the framework for innovations to occur as the aim of these policies is increasing the supply of innovations in the overall economy. Horizontal policies can further be sub-divided into two categories: (i) those dealing with improving the overall framework (sometimes referred to as the ecosystem in business literature) conditions for innovation to occur. Examples of this are science, technology and innovation policies; and (ii) specific instruments that are designed to increase the supply of innovations. Examples of this are the patents policy, the R&D tax policy, the policy on public technology procurement, direct support for R&D in the form of research grants or the policy on venture capital funding. The country, over a long period of time, has actually relied on horizontal general policies, as these are framework policies designed to hasten technological self-reliance in the country. There were four such policies starting from 1958 until 2013 (see Table 10.1). The initial policy was targeted at the production of science and not so much applied R&D. It can be argued that this was logical as the country requires scientists of a certain calibre to engage in applied and development research.

There are two common issues that all the four policies emphasized. The first is the importance of domestic technological development through investments in R&D. The more recent policies have, of course, set specific targets to be met in terms of gross expenditure on R&D (GERD) to GDP ratio. The second is the emphasis on improving the quality and quantity of scientific manpower for R&D. In fact, the more recent policies have articulated this more clearly. However, on both these issues, the actual achievements so far have fallen considerably short of what was expected. For instance, the GERD to GDP ratio has never crossed even one and the density of scientists and engineers continues to be low. Further, while the country has actually demonstrated its technological capability in industries such as the pharmaceutical, automotive and ICT, its overall technology trade balance has been negative and has been increasing over time (see Figure 10.1). This means that at the macro-level, the policies have failed to achieve their targets.

Table 10.1 Historical evolution of science and technology policies in India

Title of policy	Scope
1. Scientific Policy Resolution, 1958	To foster, promote and sustain, by all appropriate means, the cultivation of science and scientific research in all its aspects—pure, applied and educational; to ensure an adequate supply of research scientists of the highest quality within the country and to recognize their work as an important component of the strength of the nation; to encourage, and initiate, with all possible speed, programmes for the training of scientific and technical personnel, on a scale adequate to fulfil the country's needs in science and education, agriculture and industry, and defence; to ensure that men and women are encouraged that their creative talent finds full scope in scientific activity; to encourage individual initiative for the acquisition and dissemination of knowledge, and for the discovery of new knowledge in an atmosphere of academic freedom; in general, to secure for the people of the country all the benefits that can accrue from the acquisition and application of scientific knowledge. An interesting aspect of the Scientific Policy Resolution was its emphasis on creating qualified scientists and engineers.
2. Technology Policy Statement, 1983	The main aim of this policy was the country achieving technological self-reliance. It laid emphasis on domestic technological development and at the same time, acquisition of technology from abroad. The policy also aimed at adapting imported technology to local conditions, absorbing the imported technology and thereby developing local capabilities.
3. Science and Technology Policy, 2003	The policy document for the first time emphasized the promotion of innovation in the economy. For this it proposed a very comprehensive set of measures, including a policy for improving the quality and quantity of the science and engineering workforce and putting in place fiscal measures for incentivizing R&D by firms. It also proposed a target for GERD to GDP ratio to touch 2 per cent by 2006–07.
4. Science, Technology and Innovation Policy, 2013	The policy document has the aim of making India one of the five global scientific powers by 2020, establishing a world-class R&D infrastructure for gaining this global leadership, facilitating high risk innovations through new mechanisms, making careers in science, research and innovation attractive for the brightest and enhancing skills for science applications among the young (a more detailed review of this document is given later in the essay).

Source: Author's compilation based on various policy documents.

Figure 10.1 Trends in India's technology trade balance

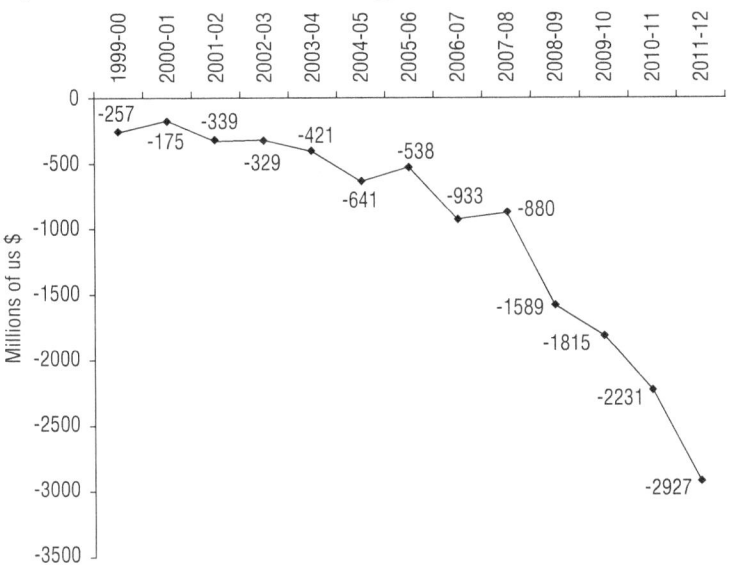

Source: Compiled from Reserve Bank of India, monthly bulletin (various issues).

Caution must be exercised in interpreting Figure 10.1, which shows worsening technological self-reliance. This is because the technology trade balance is computed by taking the difference between receipts and payments for the use of intellectual property rights (IPRs) which manifests itself in the form of royalty payments. There are reports that MNCs' affiliates operating in the country have been remitting large amounts of royalty payments to their parent companies abroad. This appears to be part of their strategy of optimizing their tax payments in India. Royalty payments attract a lower tax rate than profits which forces these firms to increase royalty payments and reduce dividend payouts. In that sense a fall in the technological balance of trade may be a statistical artefact.

On the second issue of increasing the number and quality of scientists and engineers, the situation is no better. The total stock of R&D personnel has shown a considerable increase from just 0.94 lakh as in March 1996 to 4.41 lakh as in March 2010. However, this total hides the density of scientists engaged in R&D. On a density basis, the number of researchers per million people is one of the lowest in the world as India has just 164, while China has 863, Brazil has 668 and developed countries such as Japan has 5,139 and Korea has 4,963 researchers per million people. With such a low density of R&D personnel, it is doubtful whether the country can be easily transformed to a knowledge-based economy in the near future. Further, 56 per cent of the total R&D personnel are composed of auxiliary and administrative personnel and only about 44 per cent are engaged in pure and simple R&D activities. In short, on both counts of increasing technological self-reliance and in increasing the density of scientists and engineers, the successive policies appear not to have borne any fruits.

Further, in addition to the explicit S&T policies, the National Manufacturing Policy (NMP) of 2011 had also spelt out a number of instruments for increasing investments in innovative activities by manufacturing enterprises.[2] NMP also made pronouncements on issues such as technology acquisition and development, training and skill upgradation measures and in dealing with manufacturing firms in the small and medium (SME) sector, public procurement and trade policies in as much as they affect the manufacturing sector. But on all these counts the policy does not state any schemes or measures that were not available earlier, except that it brought together separate issues under one umbrella.

Apart from these general framework policies, of late, especially over the last 10 years or so, the government has for the first time announced policies targeted at specific industries. We can identify policies with respect to automotive, biotechnology, chemicals, electronics, electrical equipment, IT services, pharmaceutical and telecommunications sectors. In other words, what one finds is a plethora of policy announcements. The aim of all these sectoral policies has been re-defining the sectoral systems of innovation in these industries in such a way that they contribute to these industries becoming more innovative. By announcing these sectoral policies, the government has affirmed the oft-repeated concern of 'one size fitting all', which is implied in the framework policies.

---

[2] For a critical review of this policy, see Mani (2011).

Evolution of the tax policy with respect to R&D

In-house or intra-mural R&D is one of the main routes through which firms innovate. In literature on the economics of innovation, it is widely recognized that if industrial R&D is left entirely in the hands of private sector enterprises, then there is a likelihood of these enterprises under-investing in R&D, which means the amount of R&D undertaken will be less than the socially desirable optimum. The tendency to under-invest is because of the problem of appropriability or the failure of private sector agents to fully appropriate the returns of their own research. Governments across the world have sought to overcome this problem by providing subsidies to private sector firms to encourage them to make continued investments in R&D. India, too, has been using tax incentives to encourage domestic enterprises to commit more resources to R&D. This policy on R&D tax incentives has evolved over time as may be seen in Table 10.2.

It is evident from Table 10.2 that India has one of the most generous incentive regimes for R&D. Generosity of a tax regime with respect to R&D is measured using a summary measure called the B-Index.[3] The lower the B-Index, the higher is the generosity of the tax regime. In fact, recent estimates of the B-Index confirm this view (see Figure 10.2).

It is evident that almost a quarter of the industrial R&D performed in India is subsidized through these tax incentives (see Table 10.3). The subsidization rate has been increasing over time when technology generation was actually globalizing.

Outcomes from a generous R&D tax regime

Has this subsidization resulted in additional investments in R&D by the business enterprise sector? To answer this question, we

---

[3] The B-is computed by the following formula: B-Index =(1- After Tax Cost)/(1-Corporate Income Tax Rate). 1- B-Index measures the tax subsidy rate. The higher the tax subsidy rate, the higher is the generosity of the tax regime.

Table 10.2 Evolution of the policy on R&D tax incentives in India

Union Budget	Major change	Scope of the change
1999–2000	R&D tax incentives of 125 per cent extended up to 2004–05	Under the current law, a weighted deduction of 125 per cent of the expenditure made on in-house R&D was available to corporate houses up to 31 March 2000. This has now been extended up to 2004–05. Further, it was proposed to extend a similar concession of permitting a weighted deduction of 125 per cent of expenditure for R&D projects entrusted to research laboratories and universities.
2000–01	This was raised to 150 per cent in the Finance Act of 2000	Under this, the incentive was available only to companies engaged in the production of drugs and pharmaceuticals, electronic equipment, computers, telecommunications equipment, chemicals, manufacture of aircraft and helicopters, automobiles and auto parts.
2009–10	R&D tax incentive extended to all industries in 2009–10	The scope of the current provision of a weighted deduction of 150 per cent on expenditure incurred on in-house R&D extended to all manufacturing businesses except for a small negative list.
2010–11	R&D tax incentive increased from 150 per cent to 200 per cent	Weighted deduction on in-house R&D expenditure increased from 150 per cent to 200 per cent. Further, the weighted deduction on payments made to national laboratories, research associations, colleges, universities and other institutions for scientific research increased from 125 per cent to 175 per cent.

Source: Author's compilation based on Union Budget documents.

need a dataset that tracks the R&D expenditures of firms that actually made use of these subsidies. Since such a dataset is hard to come by (unavailable in the public domain), as a second best, we analyse the R&D expenditure of the overall business enterprise sector (BERD). We consider two aspects of BERD: (i) Research intensity of the business enterprise sector (BERD); and (ii) Share of BERD in overall GERD.

Both indicators (i) and (ii) have shown an increase over time although some of these increases may have been due to the availability of subsidies: research intensity of the business enterprise sector doubled during this period and BERD now accounts for almost 30 per cent of GERD. Further, about two-third of BERD

Figure 10.2 Generosity of tax regimes with respect to R&D

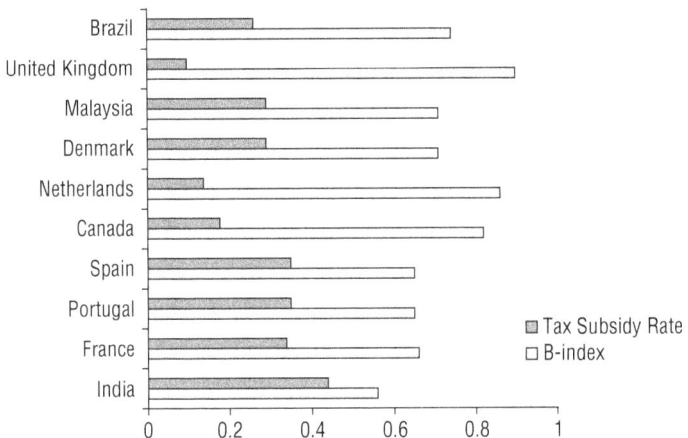

Source: Based on Stewart et al. (2012).

Table 10.3 Extent of subsidization of R&D in India

	R&D tax incentive	Business Enterprise R&D	Subsidization rate
2005–06	2839	8471.95	33.51
2006–07	1554	10485.58	14.82
2007–08	2000	12926.14	15.47
2008–09	2526	14365.46	17.58
2009–10	2416	15305.55	15.79
2010–11	4685	18332.88	25.56
2011–12	5748	21965.31	26.17

Source: Author's compilation based on Union budget documents.
Note: Values are in ₹ crore and the subsidization rate is in per cent.

is distributed across just three industries: pharmaceutical, IT and automotives and as such, the performance of R&D is not distributed across a range of industries. In fact, the concentration in the distribution of BERD has actually increased, implying that the subsidies have not really helped in spreading an R&D culture among the various industries in the manufacturing sector. The subsidies seem to have merely helped the R&D intensive industries, such as the pharmaceutical industry, to commit even more resources to R&D.

An important issue to be noted is the growth of foreign companies in R&D performance and in taking out patents based on this research both in India and abroad. Since the foreign companies are eligible to receive R&D tax benefits, they seem to have increased their R&D activities in the country. There are now a large number of foreign R&D centres[4] operating in India. The biennial R&D surveys conducted by the Department of Science and Technology and published in its Research and Development Statistics do not report R&D expenditure by MNCs separately. It has only a category called 'private sector', which may include expenditure incurred by foreign companies as well. The only source of data on R&D expenditure by foreign companies is successive surveys titled 'Finances of Foreign Direct Investment Companies'. Although the RBI has been reporting this survey for some time, it is only since 2002–03 that it has started reporting the R&D expenditure incurred by what it refers to as FDI companies which in essence are foreign companies (see Table 10.4).

An interesting fact thrown up by Table 10.4 is the growing share of foreign companies in the conduct of R&D in the country. In 2011, their share was around 29 per cent of the total BERD conducted in the country. Further, there was also a doubling of their R&D intensity during the period under consideration although for all the years it is less than that for domestic companies. In other words, foreign companies are increasingly making use of the favourable fiscal regime in the country and are performing R&D in India. While this can be a positive thing, research in this area has shown that there are very little positive externalities of the R&D efforts of foreign entities to India's economy (Basant and Mani 2012). However, an important aspect that is presently overlooked in relevant literature is the role of these foreign R&D centres as a source of a number of what are now increasingly referred to as frugal innovations (Bound and Thornton 2012).

---

[4] There are no official estimates of the number of foreign R&D centres in the country. In fact, Basant and Mani (2012) have shown that even the data on FDI in R&D released by the Secretariat of Industrial Assistance (SIA) and those by the RBI differ by a wide margin.

Table 10.4 Growing share of MNCs in the performance of business enterprise R&D in India (in per cent)

Fiscal year ending	Share of foreign companies	R&D intensity of foreign companies	R&D intensity of domestic companies
2003	10.27	0.35	0.46
2004	8.51	0.32	0.54
2005	12.99	0.29	0.62
2006	11.39	0.27	0.80
2007	15.92	0.43	0.79
2008	16.24	0.45	0.83
2009	28.24	0.71	0.85
2010	29.40	0.70	0.82
2011	28.92	0.71	

Source: Department of Science and Technology (2013) and Mani (2013).

One specific technology where there is tangible proof of this is in medical devices.[5]

An important issue to be considered is the fact that foreign companies are quick to claim an IPR over their inventions in India by seeking patents on their new inventions in the country. In fact, Mani (2010) has argued that the surge in Indian patenting in the US should be attributed to the activities of foreign R&D centres in India. The more recent updating of this data shows that during 2008 through 2012 over two-third of the patents secured by Indian inventors in the United States Patent and Trademark Office (USPTO) were granted to foreign R&D centres operating from India. These numbers can be appreciated when considering the share of foreign companies in US patenting for an earlier period (1995–99), when it was only about 16 per cent. With tighter TRIPS compliant IPR regime put in place by India, from 2005 onwards, the possibility of spill-overs to the domestic economy from the R&D done by these foreign companies stands greatly diminished.

In sum, an introduction of a more generous R&D tax regime, which is the most important policy instrument that India has put

[5] For instance, GE's Mac I, an ECG machine, is a low-cost portable unit that was developed at GE's technology centre in India to address the growing incidence of cardiovascular diseases locally.

in place to encourage R&D, appears to have increased BERD (notwithstanding comments about the availability of the right dataset), but its performance has remained concentrated in just three industries. In addition to the existence of R&D tax incentives, there are also other factors that would have driven R&D in each of these three industries like, for instance, the influence of the patent regime in the case of pharmaceuticals, export orientation in the case of IT services and the effect of competition and exports in the case of the automotive industry. Even within these industries, although we have not demonstrated the fact, R&D's performance may be concentrated in a few large firms. There is also our finding of the growth of foreign R&D centres in the country. We are, therefore, not in a position to draw any firm and unambiguous conclusions about the effect of R&D tax incentives on firm-level innovative activities.

Conclusion

The country has been trying to achieve technological self-reliance. For this a number of policies have been adopted from time to time. The implementation of these policies and monitoring of the results of specific policy instruments have not been taken in a serious manner in the country. Of the various policies, the one that is the most direct is the R&D tax policy. Our analysis of R&D expenditure and patents data shows that although the share of firms or business enterprises has increased, it is concentrated in a few industries. Further, the share of foreign companies in R&D performance is also on the increase. While there have been some successes at specific industry levels, the pharmaceutical industry being one such case, in overall terms the extent of India's technological reliance has actually worsened. It now depends far more on foreign technological inputs than ever before. Announcements of a series of policies, whether at the aggregate or at specific sectoral levels, without transliterating policies in terms of instruments, is a futile and wasteful exercise. The generous R&D tax regime is yet to show some positive effects as far as domestically owned firms are concerned. Innovative activity remains concentrated in a few industries and firms, and as such is not widespread.

References

Basant, Rakesh and Sunil Mani. (2012). 'Foreign R&D Centres in India: An Analysis of their Size, Structure and Implications', Ahmedabad: Indian Institute of Management Working Paper, WP2012-01-06.

Bound, Kirsten and Ian Thornton. (2012). *Our frugal future; Lessons from India's Innovation System,* London: Nesta. Available at: http://www.nesta.org.uk/sites/default/files/our_frugal_future.pdf; accessed on 24 January 2014.

Department of Science and Technology. (2013). *Research and Development Statistics 2011–12.* New Delhi: National Science and Technology Management Information System, Ministry of Science and Technology, Government of India. Available at: http://www.nstmis-dst.org/SnT-Indicators2011-12.aspx; accessed on 14 January 2013.

Mani, Sunil. (1995). 'Technology import and skill development in a microelectronics based industry: The case of India's electronic switching systems', in Amiya Kumar Bagchi (ed.), *New Technology and the Worker's Response, Microelectronics, Labour and Society.* New Delhi: Sage Publications, pp. 98–122.

———. (2010). 'Are innovations on rise in India since the onset of reforms of 1991?' Analysis of its evidence and some disquieting features', *International Journal of Technology and Globalization,* 5 (1 and 2): 5–42.

———. (2011). 'National Manufacturing Policy: Making India a Powerhouse?' *Economic and Political Weekly,* 46 (53): 16–19.

———. (2013). 'Policy spree or policy paralysis, An evaluation of India's efforts at encouraging firm-level innovative activities', paper presented at the national conference on 'India's industrialization: how to overcome the stagnation', Institute for Studies in Industrial Development (ISID), New Delhi, 20–21 December.

Stewart, Luke A., Jacek Warda and Robert D. Atkinson. (2012). *We're #27!: The United States Lags Far Behind in R&D Tax Incentive Generosity,* Washington, DC: The Information Technology and Innovation Foundation.

Chapter 11

Public Finance: Development, Equity and Political Economy

M. Govinda Rao*

Introduction

Public finance is concerned with the process and effects of
raising revenues and incurring expenditures by the government
for fulfilling its objectives.[1] The important objectives of public
finance are ensuring safety and security of the people, providing
competitive levels of physical and social infrastructure to accelerate
growth, ensuring wide participation in the growth process
through human development, redistributing incomes to reduce
poverty and managing the overall level of economic activity in
a stable and sustainable manner.[2] The role of the government in

* The author is thankful to Dr Pulapre Balakrishnan for detailed comments
on the earlier draft of this essay.

[1] This is also called fiscal policy. 'Fiscal' is Latin for treasury, and the policies
calibrated through the operation of treasury are called fiscal policy.

[2] Musgrave (1959) in his classic book assigns three important objectives
to budgetary policy: allocation, redistribution and stabilization. Accelerating of
economic growth is subsumed under 'allocation'.

providing competitive levels of social and physical infrastructure is particularly important in developing countries because it determines the enabling environment for private investments to create productive employment opportunities for the workforce. Indeed, the extent of government intervention through budgetary operations depends on the perceived role of the state; a minimalist government essentially provides basic public goods whereas a benevolent view of the government assigns it significant roles in redistribution and production-distribution systems. Much of the mainstream literature assumes a benevolent state and assigns the extended role of providing goods and services with externalities and undertaking significant redistribution. However, public choice theorists' view is that agents within the government (bureaucrats, politicians or other special interest groups) maximize their own gains rather than the welfare of the people and therefore, try to expand the role of the state to maximize their own benefits. They would like to restrict the role of the state to the provision of basic public goods.[3] In a democratic polity, the government is expected to play a much larger role than a minimalist government. Besides ensuring safety and security and protecting property rights, the government is also required to provide the social and physical infrastructure. Governments have the task of redistributing incomes and reducing poverty. Finally, after the Great Depression, and influenced by the Keynesian view, public spending was assigned a central role in raising the level of economic activity to ensure full employment financed by, if necessary, borrowing.

After independence, in India's public sector-dominated, heavy industry-based industrialization strategy public finance was assigned a central role. The specific objectives of the fiscal policy were raising the level of savings, particularly public savings (by generating surpluses from public enterprises), financing increasing levels of investments required to accelerate growth of the economy, influencing the magnitude and direction of economic activity as

---

[3] In a week-long symposium in the University of Munich, Musgrave and Buchanan, the two tallest stalwarts, discussed the two views threadbare and this is detailed in Buchanan and Musgrave (1999).

directed in the plans and bringing about a reduction in inequalities in income and wealth.

However, there are serious questions on the effectiveness of fiscal policy in achieving the intended tasks.[4] Although there was significant expansion of the public sector, it failed to generate the level of public savings required for investments. A considerable portion of public sector spending had to be financed from borrowings, leading to large deficits and debt. Public spending failed to create the physical and social infrastructure required to propel private investments to raise the level of economic activity required to generate productive employment and did not adequately empower the workforce through education, skill development and healthcare.

This essay analyses developments in public finance in the post-reforms era, particularly during the last decade. The next section analyses the effectiveness of tax policies in mobilizing the resources required for providing administrative, social and economic services. This is followed by an analysis of recent trends in the level and composition of public spending. The portion of public spending not financed through taxes and other non-tax revenues such as user charges and fees have to be financed by borrowing. This involves questions of inter-generational equity and could lead to problems of sustainability of public finances and stability in prices. Issues relating to deficits and debt are discussed in the next section. The last section provides concluding remarks.

Taxation

The tax policy is a major instrument through which resources are transferred from the private sector to the government for financing its expenditures. However, whenever taxes are imposed, distortions are inevitable as they affect the incentive to save, invest and undertake risks. A good tax system is supposed to raise the

---

[4] For a detailed evaluation of the fiscal policy in India's planned development strategy see Bagchi and Nayak (1994).

required revenues by minimizing the distortions. The tax system is also employed as a major instrument for bringing about the desired distribution of incomes. However, high tax rates required for redistribution create severe disincentives. Excessive rate differentiations in consumption taxes can also alter relative prices and resource allocation in unintended ways. The best approach to tax policy is to have a broad base, low rate, minimum rate differentiation and transparency. Such a tax system will raise the required revenues by minimizing the cost of collection and compliance and distortion costs.

Despite several rounds of reforms, the tax system in India has not been able to generate the required revenues and the tax revenue relative to GDP has virtually been stagnant over a long period. In the pre-reforms period, the tax–GDP ratio rose to a high of almost 16 per cent in 1989–90. Although it reached a high of 17.5 per cent in 2007–08, it declined to 16.4 per cent in 2011–12, which was only marginally higher than the ratio in 1989–90. In 1991–92 when the reforms were initiated in India, the tax-GDP ratio was 15.8 per cent, but it declined thereafter due to reduction in import duties and by 2001–02, it was 13.4 per cent.[5] The general experience of countries reducing import duties is to make up the revenue by introducing a value added tax (VAT). However, this could not be done in the Indian context as the power to levy customs duties is with the Centre and sales tax is with the states. The second round of reforms came after 2004–05 with the application of technology by way of the tax information network (TIN) and expansion of the service tax base. At the state level, replacing a cascading sales tax regime with multiple rates with a value added tax with only two rates simplified the tax system, reduced distortions and increased revenue productivity. Thus, the decline in the tax ratio during the 1990s was mainly due to a decline in revenue from customs whereas the increase in revenue during the next decade was mainly due to the sharp increase in direct tax revenue (Figure 11.1).

The tax system in India suffers from a number of shortcomings (Rao and Rao 2011). First, the revenue productivity of the tax

[5] For a detailed analysis of the Indian tax system, see Rao and Rao (2006).

Figure 11.1   Percentage of tax revenue to GDP: Direct and indirect taxes

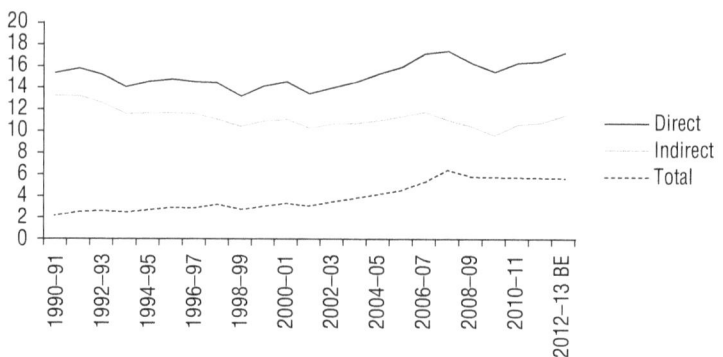

Source: Public Finance Statistics, Ministry of Finance, Government of India (September 2013).

system continues to be low. Second, narrow bases in both direct and indirect taxes cause not only low revenue productivity but also violate cannons of equity. Third, with several exemptions and concessions and multiple rates, both direct and indirect taxes in India create significant distortions in resource allocation. Finally, there are problems of tax administration, in terms of its training, capability and discretion, information system and use of technology and tax payer services. There is hardly any information exchange to ensure effective enforcement of the tax, not only between the central and state tax departments, but even between the Central Board of Direct Taxes and the Central Board of Excise and Customs.

As mentioned earlier, the tax–GDP ratio of the central and state governments, after increasing from 13.4 per cent in 2001–02 increased sharply to 17.5 per cent in 2007–08 but thereafter declined to 16.4 per cent in 2011–12. Stagnancy in revenue is seen from the fact that the ratio is only marginally higher than what it had been in 1989–90 when it was 16 per cent! The ratio is low not only from the viewpoint of the requirement for spending on physical infrastructure and human development, but even by the standards of countries with a comparable level of development. A study by Bird and Zolt (2003) shows that the average tax ratios for countries with a comparable level of development in 2002 was higher at 17 per cent whereas the ratio for India in that year was just about 14 per cent. Among the emerging economies, Russia has the highest tax–GDP ratio of over 36 per cent, followed by Brazil with over 33 per cent and South Africa with 25 per cent.

Second, both central and state taxes suffer from the disadvantage of narrow bases despite several rounds of reforms. This not only causes low productivity but also violates equity. As discussed by the Task Force on Direct Taxes (Government of India 2002), the assignment of taxes on agricultural income to the states and non-agricultural income to the Centre has provided an easy avenue for many high income earners to avoid and evade paying taxes. The states on their part have not been able to levy tax on agricultural incomes due to strong interest groups. Special interest group politics is also responsible for wide-ranging exemptions and concessions, which significantly erode the bases of both central and state taxes. Tax preferences are given ostensibly in pursuit of various objectives such as enclave development (such as special economic zones), providing infrastructure, regional development and promoting small-scale industry. The pursuit of these objectives, besides narrowing the tax bases, has complicated the tax structure, provided scope for rent seeking by tax officials and increased compliance costs.

The proposed enactment of the Direct Taxes Code (DTC) and the implementation of a Goods and Services Tax (GST) are meant to broaden the base and simplify the tax system but it remains to be seen how the reforms will unwind. Even after two drafts of the DTC were put out for discussion as far back as in 2009 and 2011, not much progress has been made. GST reforms are supposed to unify a number of domestic trade taxes, expand the base, provide a comprehensive input tax credit and completely relieve the taxes on exports at both central and state levels. They are also supposed to transform the tax system into a destination-based consumption tax by abolishing inter-state sales tax. However, the challenges are formidable. Besides amending the Constitution to empower the Centre to levy taxes beyond the manufacturing level and the states to levy taxes on services, agreements are necessary on thresholds, items to be exempted, the rate structure, administrative system, the mechanism to relieve the tax on inter-state trade, enforcement of agreements, dispute resolution mechanisms and scheme for compensating revenue losses.

Third, the tax system has not adequately served the objective of equity. As already mentioned, the various exemptions and concessions violate the principle of equal treatment of equals. Two persons with identical incomes pay different taxes due to exemptions of and concessions on income from some sources or uses. The redistribution in taxation has to be mainly achieved through the direct tax system. However, even as the share of direct taxes in total tax revenue has shown an increase over the years, its impact on overall redistribution is negligible. Only 3 per cent of the population pays personal income tax and 89 per cent of the tax payers pay less than ₹5 lakh and those paying more than ₹20 lakh constitute just about 1.3 per cent of the tax payers. It is surprising that the number of tax payers with incomes more than ₹1 crore is just about 42,800.

Public expenditure

Public expenditure in India as a ratio to GDP does not show a clear long-term trend. In 1990–91, it was 26.7 per cent and even in 2011–12, it was broadly at the same level. However, if a shorter period is taken, it is seen that the public expenditure–GDP ratio declined from 25.8 per cent in 2000–01 to 24.4 per cent in 2007–08 before increasing to 26.8 per cent in 2011–12. Similar trends are seen in the case of central and state government expenditures. Central government expenditure, which was a little over 11 per cent of GDP from 2000–01 to 2007–08, increased to 12.4 per cent in 2009–10, but thereafter declined to 11.8 per cent in 2011–12. A major part of the increase after 2007–08 was in revenue expenditures mainly due to pre-election decisions to revise the pay scales of government employees, farm loan waivers and expansion in the coverage of the rural employment guarantee scheme from 200 districts to the whole country in 2008–09. There was also a large subsidy outgo due to political difficulties in increasing the administered price of distillates in tune with an increase in the international price of crude oil. Capital expenditures as a ratio of GDP continued to hover around 4 per cent. State-level public expenditures relative to GDP declined from 14.6 per cent in 2000–01 to 13.8 per cent in 2007–08 before increasing to 15.1 per cent in 2011–12.

An analysis of public spending in India shows that the allocation for essential social services and physical infrastructure is low by international standards. At about 1.3 per cent of GDP, spending on health and family welfare is very low. According to the Human Development Report (2013), even in the least developed countries, public health expenditure was 1.7 per cent of GDP in 2010. The situation is not very different in the case of education. Relative to GDP, expenditure on education in 2011–12 was just about 3.5 per cent and this is much lower than the expenditures in countries with comparable levels of development.

Competitiveness of domestic producers depends on the quality of physical infrastructure available, but the trend in public spending on this is not very different. Capital expenditure by the central government as a ratio to GDP, in fact, declined from about 4 per cent in 2003–04 to 1.8 per cent in 2011–12 and much of the increase seen in capital expenditure was actually at the state level. The aggregate capital expenditure of state governments increased during the period from a little over 0.5 per cent to about 2.2 per cent. At the central level, capital expenditure as a ratio of GDP declined from 2.4 per cent in 2007–08 to 1.7 per cent in 2012–13 mainly due to stagnant revenues on the one hand and sharply increasing subsidies and transfers crowding out capital expenditures on the other. Thus, political dynamics resulted in capital expenditures taken as a residual.

An important development is the significant increase in subsidies and transfers. At the central level alone, subsides as a ratio to GDP more than doubled from 1.2 per cent in 2000–01 to 2.5 per cent in 2012–13. In the coming years, food security is likely to claim substantial additional allocation. In addition, there has been a significant increase in transfers such as for employment guarantee, nutritional schemes and assistance for construction of houses (Indira Awas Yojana). At the state level too, there has been a proliferation of various subsidies and transfers which even include giving away television sets, laptops and food processors and grinders. In contrast, as mentioned earlier, spending on healthcare and education including skill development has not shown any increase. Capital expenditure to strengthen physical infrastructure at the Centre has shown a decline since 2007–08. Thus, the focus of the poverty alleviation strategy seems to be a short-run appeasement of the poor by giving them consumption entitlements rather than a long-term policy of ensuring empowerment, skill development and employability.

Another important development in the political economy of public spending is the intrusion of central government into subjects reserved for the states in the Constitution. With the coalition government at the Centre having regional parties as its pivotal members, there is pressure on spending more on state subjects. At the same time, there are states ruled by regional parties that are unfavourable to the central government. In order to take the credit and claim ownership, the central government designs programmes and gives grants to the states using them merely as implementing agencies or gives these grants directly to implementing agencies bypassing the states to claim ownership for these programmes. For example, in 2011–12 grants for centrally sponsored schemes constituted 19 per cent of central government expenditures; while the states were given 10.5 per cent, grants given directly to spending agencies amounted to 8.4 per cent of central expenditures. Over the years, there has been a proliferation of centrally sponsored schemes and giving grants to implementing agencies bypassing the states, which was negligible in 2001–02, became particularly pronounced in recent years.

From the viewpoint of regional equity, the distribution of state-level expenditures is extremely important. An analysis shows that inter-state differences in per capita spending on social and economic services are high and have been increasing over the years. Although since 2003–04, the growth in expenditures in low per capita income states has been higher than that in advanced states, per capita expenditures on these services continue to diverge. In 2011–12, for example, per capita development expenditure in Bihar, the lowest per capita income state at ₹4,900 was only 66 per cent of the average of per capita expenditures on these services in general category states. In fact, per capita developmental expenditures in Haryana (the state with the highest per capita income) were 2.4 times that of Bihar. This means that if the unit cost of providing these services is the same, developmental services for citizens in Haryana will be 2.4 times those in Bihar. Similar differences are seen in the case of education, healthcare and economic services (Panagariya et al. 2014). The reason for this can be found in the sharp inter-state differences in the capacity to raise revenues and the inability of the transfer system to offset revenue disabilities.

Public finances: Deficits and debt

Budgetary policy is an important factor determining the level of economic activity. While public spending increases aggregate demand, taxes levied to finance it reduce demand. Even when the increase in government expenditure is fully financed by taxes, creating additional infrastructure can enhance productivity and trigger additional investments leading to higher employment and incomes. Similarly, additional public spending financed from borrowings when the private sector fails to generate sufficient demand to achieve full employment, can raise the level of economic activity to increase employment and incomes. In developing economies, high public spending financed by borrowing or even by money creation is considered desirable if it results in a net increase in economic activity resulting in higher employment and incomes. However, if it does not result in a net increase in incomes, higher spending financed by money creation could cause inflation.

While generally speaking, public spending financed by borrowings is necessary, it is important to ensure that it leads to additional economic activity. In normal times, the golden rule is that all current expenditures for paying salaries, interest, maintaining capital assets, subsidies and other transfers should be financed from current revenues from tax and non-tax sources while capital expenditures may be financed by borrowing. However, since it is not possible to give a general rule on the optimal level of deficits and debt, borrowings may be resorted to so long as they lead to a net increase in employment and incomes. But excessive borrowings can have severe adverse implications. First, these could put upward pressure on interest rates and crowd-out private investments. Second, a high volume of debt results in large interest payments which pre-empts public spending on productive activities. Third, borrowings now will have to be repaid later through higher taxes and therefore, involve a burden for future generations. Fourth, high deficits could lead to balance of payment problems (Rangarajan and Srivastava 2005). For these reasons credit-rating agencies assign high risk perceptions to countries with high levels of deficits and debt. Therefore, in many countries, fiscal rules are legislated to contain deficit and debt levels.

In India, there have been concerns about deficits and debt for long and the economic crisis of 1991 has been attributed to a lax fiscal policy. As Little and Joshi (1994: 215) state, '...the crisis of 1990/91 and 1991/92 is wholly attributable to the lax fiscal policy of the preceding years. The rapid growth of debt, ... together with political instability that delayed effective response to the gathering storm, made it impossible to finance the balance of payments deficit.' The large fiscal deficit resurfaced in 2001–02 when the consolidated fiscal deficit was 10.3 per cent of GDP, primary deficit was close to 3 per cent and the revenue deficit was about 7 per cent. With the outstanding liabilities of the government estimated at 72.5 per cent of GDP and interest payment claiming 35 per cent of the total revenue receipts, there were serious questions about debt sustainability.[6] Consequently, the central government passed the Fiscal Responsibility and Budget Management (FRBM) Act in 2003 and this was followed by all the states enacting fiscal responsibility legislations based on the recommendation of the 12th Finance Commission. The commission set targets for phasing

---

[6] According to the Domar rule, when the primary deficit is zero, debt is sustainable if the GDP rate of growth is higher than the effective interest rate on borrowing. With the primary deficit hovering at around 2–3 per cent of GDP, there were a number of years when the debt–GDP ratio showed a steady increase. See Buiter and Patel (2006).

out revenue deficits at both central and state levels and contain the fiscal deficit at 3 per cent each at the central and state levels (Government of India 2004).

The period 2004–05 to 2007–08 saw significant fiscal consolidation at both the central and state levels (Table 11.1; Figure 11.2). Buoyed by sharp acceleration in a growth of revenues, the fiscal deficit to GDP ratio at the Centre declined from over 6 per cent in 2001–02 to 3 per cent in 2007–08. Income tax revenues alone increased from 3.7 per cent of GDP in 2003–04 to 6.3 per cent of GDP in 2007–08. Despite this, the central government could not phase out the revenue deficit, even as it declined from 4.4 per cent of GDP in 2001–02 to 1.1 per cent in 2007–08. In contrast, the states were able to completely phase out the revenue deficit by 2007–08 and contain their fiscal deficit at 1.5 per cent. Thus, by 2007–08, relative to GDP, the consolidated revenue deficit GDP was just about 4.5 per cent as against a target of 6 per cent, revenue deficit was just about half a per cent and there was a primary surplus of 1 per cent.

Although the states in the aggregate continued to observe fiscal discipline, the central government's fiscal position changed completely after 2008–09 mainly due to sharp increases in subsidies and transfers. The extension of the Mahatma Gandhi

Figure 11.2 Fiscal deficit in India: Centre and states (per cent of GDP)

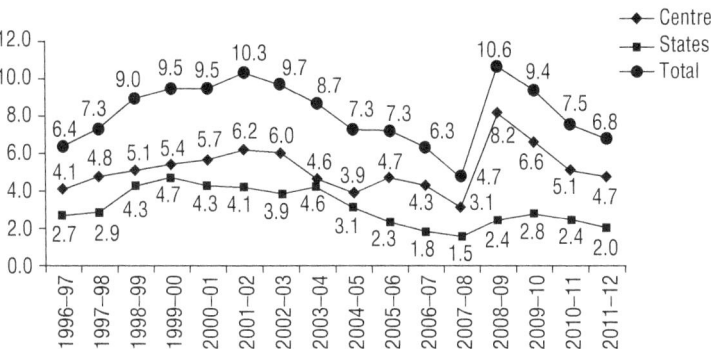

Source: Public Finance Statistics, Ministry of Finance, Government of India (September 2013).

Table 11.1 Deficit in India: Centre, states and consolidated

	Centre			States			Consolidated		
	Revenue Deficit	Fiscal Deficit	Primary Deficit	Revenue Deficit	Fiscal Deficit	Primary Deficit	Revenue Deficit	Fiscal Deficit	Primary Deficit
2000–01	4.1	5.7	0.9	2.5	4.3	1.8	6.6	9.5	3.7
2001–02	4.4	6.2	1.5	2.7	4.1	1.4	7.0	10.3	2.9
2002–03	4.4	6.0	1.1	2.3	3.9	1.3	6.6	9.7	3.0
2003–04	3.6	4.6	0.0	2.2	4.3	1.5	5.8	8.7	1.9
2004–05	2.4	3.9	0.0	1.2	3.1	0.7	3.5	7.3	1.1
2005–06	2.5	4.7	0.4	0.2	2.3	0.2	2.7	7.3	0.8
2006–07	1.9	4.3	-0.2	-0.6	1.8	-0.4	1.3	6.3	-0.3
2007–08	1.1	3.1	-0.9	-0.9	1.5	-0.5	0.2	4.7	-1.0
2008–09	4.5	8.2	2.6	-0.2	2.4	0.6	4.3	10.6	3.4
2009–10	5.2	6.5	3.1	2.0	2.8	1.0	5.5	9.4	4.1
2010–11	3.2	4.8	1.8	0.2	2.4	0.8	3.6	7.2	2.7
2011–12	4.4	5.7	2.7	-0.1	2.3	-1.6	4.3	8.0	1.1
2012–13	3.9	5.2	2.0	-0.4	2.1	-1.9	3.5	8.7	0.9

Source: Public Finance Statistics, Ministry of Finance, Government of India (September 2013).

Rural Employment Guarantee Scheme from 200 districts to the whole country, farm-loan waiver and implementation of the Pay Commission's recommendations in the 2008–09 budget increased the central government's expenditures significantly. In addition, with oil prices hitting an all-time high of US$ 143/barrel and the government's reluctance to increase the prices of distillates in an election year, the oil marketing companies had to be compensated. Consequently, an additional subsidy bill of about 2.5 per cent of GDP on this account alone had to be met. In the event, the Centre's revenue deficit increased from 1.1 per cent in 2007–08 to 4.5 per cent in 2008–09 and the fiscal deficit increased by from 3.1 per cent to 8.2 per cent. The problem was further exacerbated by a decline in the centre's tax–GDP ratio by more than two percentage points to GDP from 11.8 per cent in 2007–08 to 9.6 per cent in 2010–11. Consequently, the consolidated revenue and fiscal deficits in 2008–09 increased to 4.4 per cent and 10.6 per cent respectively.

The government claimed fiscal expansion as a stimulus measure for combating the global financial crisis though the decisions for expansion were taken in Budget 2008–09 presented in February 2008 whereas, the crisis broke out in September 2008. In any case, the expansionary measures worked as a stimulus and not surprisingly, the Indian economy started reviving within three quarters of the crisis. However, as much of the expansion was in consumption-related expenditures and a significant proportion of the expansion was irreversible, the problem of large revenue and fiscal deficits continued to persist at the Centre, though the states continued to adhere to deficit targets.

Subsequent years have seen attempts at the central level for containing deficits partly by compressing capital expenditures and partly by lowering the oil subsidy. There was considerable windfall gain in 2010–11 from auctioning spectrum waves and this reduced the Centre's fiscal deficit to 4.8 per cent of GDP in 2010–11 and consolidated fiscal deficit to 7.2 per cent of GDP in the same year. However, this position was reversed in 2011–12 and high revenue and fiscal deficits resurfaced. This has had adverse effects on the growth rate, current account deficits as well as on the inflation rate.

Concluding remarks

Policies relating to public finance can play an important role in accelerating growth, promoting human development and reducing poverty. Public finance creates an enabling environment for investments and growth by ensuring safety and security and creating physical infrastructure. By ensuring access to education, healthcare and skill development, public spending policy enables the poor to participate and gain from the growth process through productive employment. Such a policy is particularly important for reaping the demographic dividend in an economy with a large proportion of people in the working age and a considerable proportion of them with very low education and skill levels. However, public spending has to be financed either from taxation or borrowings.

Special interest group politics has not only constrained the revenue productivity of the tax system but has also created unintended distortions. Both income as well as consumption taxes at the central and state levels suffer from narrow bases and there are strong political economy reasons for this. Assigning agricultural income tax to the states and taxes on non-agricultural income to the Centre has created an important avenue for avoidance and evasion. A strong farm lobby has ensured that the states do not levy tax on agricultural incomes and this makes detection of misclassification of non-agricultural income difficult. Various special interest groups have been able to get a variety of tax exemptions and concessions, ostensibly to fulfil a variety of objectives and this has resulted in narrowing the tax bases of direct as well as indirect taxes at both the central and state levels. This has not only reduced the tax system's revenue productivity but has also has created unintended distortions in resource allocation.

Special interest group politics has impacted on the level and composition of public expenditures as well. The low level of taxes has constrained the ability of the governments to spend adequately on social and economic services. After spending on interest payments, administration and defence, revenues available for spending on physical infrastructure and human development have been inadequate. Further, more recently the proliferation of subsidies and transfers has crowded out capital expenditures. Another important feature of public expenditure in India is inadequate allocation to human development. The government has failed to provide adequate resources to education, skill development and healthcare, which are necessary for realizing the demographic dividend.

Large and persisting deficits and debt have been a major problem in India and attempts at reducing these have not been successful, particularly at the central level. Interest payments pre-empted over 25 per cent of total revenues in 2011–12. Further, it is asserted that the large draft on the household sector's financial savings for public spending has put pressure on interest rates, adversely impacted economic growth and put pressure on the balance of payments. The large and persisting deficit has also reduced the scope for reducing interest rates to promote investment and growth by the Reserve Bank of India.

There have been concerns about deficits and debt for long. In 2001–02, the fiscal deficit was the highest at both the central and state levels. The subsequent period saw partially successful attempts at achieving fiscal consolidation largely due to faster growth of revenues and by 2007–08, the fiscal deficit targets set by the FRBM Act had been achieved at both the central and state levels. However, in the subsequent period, with subsidies and transfers registering fast growth and with the slowing economy decelerating the growth of revenues, there was a reversal in the fiscal situation. Even as state governments have, by and large, adhered to fiscal discipline and have conformed to fiscal targets, the central government has failed to conform to the fiscal rules set by the FRBM Act.

The recent experience of fiscal adjustment brings to the fore the need for a robust institutional arrangement for monitoring the central government's fiscal behaviour . While the Centre has ample powers and mechanisms to impose fiscal discipline on the states, there is no such mechanism to enforce discipline on the central government. Some countries have set up fiscal councils to monitor adherence to fiscal discipline and submit periodic reports to the legislatures but while this could help in raising awareness about the problem, ultimately it is political will that is necessary for a stable and sustainable public finance policy in India.

References

Bagchi, Amaresh and Pulin Nayak. (1994). 'A Survey of Public Finance and the Planning Process: The Indian Experience', in Amaresh Bagchi and Nicholas Stern (eds), *Tax Policy and Planning in Developing Countries*. New Delhi: Oxford University Press, pp. 21–86.

Bird, Richard and Eric Zolt. (2003). 'Introduction to Tax Policy Design and Development', paper presented at the course on Practical Issues of Tax Policy in Developing Countries, the World Bank, 28 April–1 May.

Buchanan, James and Richard A. Musgrave. (1999). *Public Finance and Public Choice*. Cambridge, Massachusetts: The MIT Press.

Buiter, Willem and Urjit Patel. (2006). 'Excessive Budget Deficits. A Government-Abused Financial System and Fiscal Rules', *India Policy Forum,* NCAER and Brookings Institution, pp. 1–54.

Government of India. (2002). *Report of the Task Force on Direct Taxes*. New Delhi: Ministry of Finance, Government of India.

———. (2004). *Report of the Finance Commission*. New Delhi: Ministry of Finance, Government of India.

Little, I.M.D and Vijay Joshi. (1994). *India: Macroeconomics and Political Economy 1964–1991*. New Delhi: Oxford University Press.

Musgrave, Richard M. (1959). *The Theory of Public Finance*. New York: Mc-Graw Hill Book Company.

Panagariya, Arvind, Pinaki Chakraborty and M. Govinda Rao. (2014). *State Level Reforms, Growth, and Development in Indian States*. New York: Oxford University Press.

Rao, M. Govinda and Kavita Rao. (2006). 'Trends and Issues in Tax Policy and Reform in India', *India Policy Forum*, NCAER and Brookings Institution 2: 55–122.

———. (2011). 'Tax System Reform in India', in Roger Gordon and Joseph Stiglitz (eds), *Tax Policy and Reform in Developing Countries*. New York: Columbia University Press.

Rangarajan C. and D. K. Srivastava. (2005). 'Fiscal Deficits and Government Debt in India: Implications for Growth and Stabilization', Working Paper No. 35, National Institute of Public Finance and Policy.

Chapter 12

Monetary Policy:
Managing Inflation, Fostering Growth

*Deepak Mohanty**

In an economy, the government and institutions strive together to optimize social welfare through policies and practices. Economic policy is, therefore, set to achieve inclusive economic growth with stability. Various facets of economic policy at times may seem to have different objectives but they are all driving towards the same destination. Fiscal policy and monetary policy are the two key instruments for attaining socioeconomic objectives. In this essay, I discuss how monetary policy in India aims to achieve the broader objectives of public policy. In particular I cover the objectives, framework and implementation of monetary policy. I also analyse the role of monetary policy in financial stability and review recent developments in terms of policy outcomes before concluding with some thoughts on monetary governance.

---

* The views expressed in this essay are personal.

Objectives of monetary policy

Monetary policy is an arm of public policy. It thus has set objectives and priorities, which are derived from the respective mandates of central banks. These range from a single objective of price stability, considered to be the dominant objective of monetary policy, to multiple objectives that also include growth and financial stability.

In the Indian context, the preamble to the Reserve Bank of India Act, 1934 delineates the basic functions of the Reserve Bank of India (RBI) as, 'to regulate the issue of Bank notes and keeping of reserves with a view to securing monetary stability in India and generally to operate the currency and credit system of the country to its advantage.' The objectives of monetary policy which evolved from this broad guideline are maintaining price stability and ensuring adequate flow of credit to the productive sectors of the economy. Monetary stability cannot be ensured without safeguarding the purchasing power of the currency. Similarly, the credit system helps foster growth, which could reinforce monetary stability. Hence, stabilization of inflation at a low level and stabilization of output around its potential level remain the quintessential objectives of monetary policy in most countries. In practice, monetary policy in India endeavoured to maintain a judicious balance between economic growth and price stability.

It is easy to define inflation as most people feel it: you need more and more money over time to buy the same quantity and quality of goods and services. It is, however, not easy to define potential output. It is generally understood as full employment output. For a country like ours with so much surplus labour, full employment output is very high. But there are several constraints such as skills and resources in achieving this over the medium-term. Hence, we have to distinguish between aspirational growth rates and what is feasible in a non-inflationary manner over the medium-term. Price stability, therefore, is not an end in itself but a means of achieving high output growth in a sustainable manner.

Price stability does not necessarily mean a constant price level, but a low and stable inflation. This is because both high inflation and deflation impose costs on the economy by way of loss of output and misallocation of resources. However, it is difficult to define the precise level of low and stable inflation. In practice, inflation targets range from 2 per cent for developed countries to 3.5 per cent for developing countries which have come to be understood as price stability (Schmitt-Grohe et al. 2011).

For India, the Chakravarty Committee (1985) defined an annual inflation rate of 4 per cent as the tolerable level. In this context, the notion of a threshold level of inflation, which is the inflexion point in the growth-inflation trade-off, becomes important. Beyond the threshold, inflation by itself becomes inimical to growth. Recent studies on India suggest that the threshold inflation could be in the range of 4–6 per cent (Mohanty et al. (2011) Pattanaik and Nadhanael (2011). However, the inflation threshold need not necessarily be the target of monetary policy. In fact, the inflation objective or the target level of inflation for monetary policy should be lower than the inflation threshold, considering the existence of significant lags in the transmission of monetary policy measures and the costs of inflation.

Costs of inflation

Inflation, though a nominal variable, imposes real costs on the economy. Let me elaborate.

First, inflation erodes the value of money. India is a moderate inflation country with the post-independent period 62-year long-term average inflation rate being 6.7 per cent, notwithstanding occasional spikes. Yet during this period, the overall price level has multiplied 45 times. This means that ₹100 now is worth only ₹2.2 at 1950–51 prices. Since price stability is a key objective of monetary policy, central banks are obviously concerned with inflation.

Second, high and persistent inflation imposes significant socioeconomic costs. Given that the burden of inflation is disproportionately large on the poor, and considering that India has a large informal sector, high inflation by itself can lead to distributional inequality. Therefore, for a welfare-oriented public policy, low inflation becomes a critical element for ensuring balanced progress.

Third, high inflation distorts economic incentives by diverting resources away from productive investment to speculative activities. Fixed-income earners and pensioners see a decline in their disposable incomes and standard of living. Inflation reduces households' savings as they try to maintain the real value of their consumption. The consequent fall in overall investment in the economy reduces its potential growth. With a high inflation of over four years we are already seeing a fall in household savings in financial assets, particularly in bank deposits. At the same time households' preference for gold has increased. This is putting additional pressure on our balance of payments (BoP).

Fourth, economic agents base their consumption and investment decisions on their current and expected future incomes as well as their expectations on future inflation rates. Persistent high inflation alters inflationary expectations and apprehensions arising from price uncertainty do lead to a cut in spending by individuals and a slowdown in investment by corporates, which hurts economic growth in the long run.

Fifth, as inflation rises and turns volatile, it raises the inflation risk premia in financial transactions. Hence, nominal interest rates tend to be higher than they would have been under low and stable inflation.

Sixth, if domestic inflation remains persistently higher than that of the trading partners, it affects external competitiveness through appreciation of the real exchange rate.

Finally, as inflation rises beyond a threshold, it has an adverse impact on overall growth. The RBI's technical assessment suggests that the threshold level of inflation for India is in the range of 4 to 6 per cent. If inflation persists beyond this level, it could lower economic growth over the medium term.

In fact, the average inflation during the 2000s was around 5.5 per cent. However, near double-digit inflation persisting since the beginning of 2010–11 has been posing a challenge for monetary policy in India. Notwithstanding this recent inflation upsurge, the objective of monetary policy is reducing inflation to 5 per cent in the short run and 3 per cent over the medium term.

The recent global financial crisis has, however, shown that low levels of inflation and high levels of growth do not guarantee financial stability. Accordingly, there is an increasing emphasis that financial stability should also be an explicit objective of central banks besides price stability and growth. In India, however, financial stability was recognized as another important objective of monetary policy much before the crisis.

Thus, monetary policy in India has evolved to have multiple objectives of price stability, growth and financial stability. These objectives are not inherently contradictory, but rather, they are mutually reinforcing. This is so as price and financial stability are important for sustaining a high level of growth, which is the ultimate objective of public policy.

Monetary policy framework

Achieving the objectives of monetary policy requires articulation of a consistent monetary policy framework. This becomes necessary as central banks strive to achieve these objectives only indirectly through instruments which are under their direct control. A monetary policy framework, however, has been a continuously evolving process contingent upon the level of development of financial markets and institutions as also the degree of global integration. Let me give you a snapshot of the evolution of our monetary policy framework and operations since the inception of the RBI in 1935.

First, in the formative years during 1935–50, the focus of monetary policy was on regulating the supply of and demand for credit in the economy through the bank rate, reserve requirements and open market operations (OMO). Through the bank rate, the RBI could signal the stance of monetary policy and could also alter the cost of money in the economy. By altering the cash reserve ratio (CRR)—the ratio of cash that the banks are statutorily required to hold with the RBI in relation to broadly their deposit liabilities—

the RBI could control money supply. Similarly, the RBI could alter the liquidity in the system through OMO—by buying and selling of government securities.

Second, during the development phase during 1951–70, the need for supporting plan financing through accommodation of government deficit financing by the RBI began to significantly influence the conduct of monetary policy. This led to the introduction of several quantitative control measures to contain the consequent inflationary pressures while ensuring credit to preferred sectors. These measures included selective credit control, the credit authorization scheme (CAS) and 'social control' measures to enhance the flow of credit to priority sectors. The bank rate was raised more frequently during this period.

Third, during 1971–90, the focus of monetary policy was on credit planning. However, the dominance of fiscal policy over monetary policy accentuated and continued through the 1980s. To raise resources from banks for the government the statutory liquidity ratio (SLR) was progressively increased from the statutory minimum then of 25 per cent of banks' net demand and time liabilities (NDTL) in February 1970 to 38.5 per cent by September 1990. And to neutralize the inflationary impact of deficit financing, CRR was gradually raised from its statutory minimum of 3 per cent to 15 per cent of NDTL during the period.

Fourth, the 1980s saw the adoption of a monetary targeting framework based on the recommendations of the Chakravarty Committee (1985). Under this framework, reserve money was used as the operating target, and broad money (M_3) as an intermediate target. A number of money market instruments such as inter-bank participation certificates (IBPCs), certificates of deposit (CDs) and Commercial Paper (CP) were introduced based on the recommendations of the Vaghul Committee (1987).

Fifth, structural reforms and financial liberalization in the 1990s led to a shift in the financing paradigm for the government and commercial sectors with increasingly market-determined interest rates and exchange rate. By the second half of the 1990s, the RBI was able to move away from direct instruments to indirect market-based instruments in its liquidity management operations.

The CRR and SLR had been brought down to 9.5 per cent and 25 per cent of NDTL of banks by 1997.

Sixth, on account of measures undertaken during the 1990s for developing various segments of the financial market, there was discernible deepening of the financial sector. This significantly improved the effectiveness in the transmission of policy signals through indirect instruments such as interest rates. Recognizing the challenges posed by financial liberalization and the growing complexities of monetary management, the RBI switched to a multiple indicator approach in 1998–99.

Under the multiple indicator approach, while broad money continued to remain an information variable, greater emphasis was placed on rate channels for formulating monetary policy. A host of macroeconomic indicators including interest rates or rates of return in different segments of financial markets, along with other indicators on currency, credit by banks and financial institutions, fiscal position, trade, capital flows, inflation rate, exchange rate, refinancing and transactions in foreign exchange available on a high frequency basis were juxtaposed with output data for drawing implications for forming monetary policy. As a result, monetary policy operations became more broad-based on diverse sets of information and provided flexibility in the conduct of monetary management.

Finally, the multiple indicators approach continued to evolve and was further augmented by forward-looking indicators and a panel of parsimonious time series models. The forward-looking indicators were drawn from the RBI's industrial outlook survey, capacity utilization survey, professional forecasters' survey and inflation expectations survey. The assessment from these indicators and models fed into the projection of growth and inflation. Simultaneously, the RBI also gives a projection for broad money (M_3), which serves as an important information variable, so as to make the resource balance in the economy consistent with the credit needs of the government and the private sector. Thus, the current framework of monetary policy can be termed as an augmented multiple indicator approach. Let me now turn to the nuts and bolts of monetary policy.

Implementation of monetary policy

For effective implementation of monetary policy, the monetary policy framework needs a supporting operating procedure. An operating procedure is defined as day-to-day management of monetary conditions consistent with the overall stance of monetary policy. Generally, it involves: (i) defining an operational target, generally an interest rate; (ii) setting a policy rate which could influence the operational target; (iii) setting the width of the corridor for short-term market interest rates; (iv) conducting liquidity operations to keep the operational target interest rate stable within the corridor; and (v) signalling of policy intentions.

As with the monetary policy framework, the corresponding operating procedure has also been an evolving process in India. Applying CRR on banks' liabilities and OMO has traditionally been the instrument of monetary policy. But with the introduction of the liquidity adjustment facility (LAF) in 2004, overnight management of systemic liquidity at the desired interest rate emerged as the most active instrument of monetary policy. LAF's various features have undergone several modifications to enhance the effectiveness of monetary operations, the most recent major changes being in May 2011.

The new operating procedure introduced in May 2011 retained the essential features of the earlier LAF framework with some key modifications. First, the weighted average overnight call money rate was explicitly recognized as the operating target of monetary policy. Second, the repo rate was made the only one independently varying policy rate. Third, a new marginal standing facility (MSF) was instituted under which scheduled commercial banks (SCBs) could borrow overnight up to 1 per cent of their respective NDTL at 100 basis points above the repo rate at their discretion. Fourth, the revised corridor was defined with a fixed width of 200 basis points. The repo rate was placed in the middle of the corridor, with the reverse repo rate 100 basis points below it and the MSF rate 100 basis points above it.

Consequently, the transmission of monetary policy in terms of the movement in the call money market interest rate has shown improvement. It has also been observed that money market interest rates are better aligned after the implementation of the new operating framework. Further, better transmission to the debt market segment is also evident from closer alignment between rates on debt market instruments and call rates. Transmission to the credit market is much more complex and occurs through the cost channel. Banks respond to policy changes by altering deposit rates depending on liquidity conditions and credit demand. As the cost of deposits rises alongside money market rates, lending rates respond to policy rate changes with a lag. Let me now briefly discuss how the RBI formulates monetary policy.

Policy formulation processes

Given the monetary policy framework and the corresponding operating procedure, a process is followed in forming policy. The process of forming monetary policy in India had traditionally been largely internal with only the end-product of actions being made public. The process has, over time, become more consultative and participative with an external orientation. The process leading to monetary policy actions entails a wide range of inputs involving the internal staff, market participants, academics, financial market experts and the RBI's board.

Within the RBI, the work process has been re-oriented to focus on technical analysis, coordination and more market orientation. The three concerned research departments provide independent technical inputs and assessment in the monetary policy strategy meeting chaired by the Governor and attended by the top management. Given the inherent complexity of macroeconomic management, diversity of viewpoints helps avoid the pitfalls of groupthink.

Since banks are a major counterpart of the RBI, pre-policy consultations through resource management discussions are held with commercial banks, which together account for more than three-fourths of the banking business. In addition, in the financial sector, consultations are held with the Indian Banks Association

(IBA), urban and rural cooperative banks/credit associations and association of non-banking financial companies. In the real sector, consultations are held with national-level trade associations. Consultations are also held with select economists and senior economic journalists to ascertain their reading of the economic situation and policy recommendations.

In keeping with international best practices, the RBI has constituted a technical advisory committee (TAC) on monetary policy with outside experts, though its role remains advisory. In order to enhance transparency, TAC's deliberations and policy recommendations are released to the public within four weeks of such meetings. However, the Governor of the RBI is the ultimate authority to take decisions on monetary policy matters.

There are several other standing and ad hoc committees or groups which play a critical role with regard to policy advice. An interdepartmental Financial Markets Committee (FMC) focuses on day-to-day market operations and tactics on an ongoing basis. The whole range of consultations and technical analysis enable the Governor to make the best possible decision under the circumstances besides enhancing the transparency of the policymaking process. In addition, the Governor and the top management of the RBI set out the rationale for policy decisions through quarterly policy statements, mid-quarter reviews, press interviews and speeches.

While forming monetary policy is a technical process, it has evolved into a highly consultative and participative process. This not only enhances its transparency but policy decisions also become informed with the analysis and viewpoints of the concerned stakeholders. As many outcomes in modern market-based economies are guided by expectations, a consultative process also helps in managing expectations.

Transparency in monetary policy and its communication in India have evolved with global thinking in the matter. Earlier, monetary policy decisions by central banks were often shrouded in mystery. Secrecy was considered a virtue. It was believed that monetary policy could be more effective by surprising the markets. This thinking has changed completely. Now central banks believe in not surprising the market, making available all information that goes into a policy decision and coming out in the public to explain their policy decisions. An essential feature of the inflation targeting framework, that many central banks have adopted, is transparency and communication. Though the RBI is not a formal inflation targeting central bank, it has increasingly embraced the best features of such a framework. Being a public institution, the RBI is accountable. Greater transparency and better communication can only reinforce the accountability mechanism in a democracy. Let me now turn to the interface between monetary policy and financial stability.

Monetary policy and financial stability

As mentioned earlier, the evolution of monetary policy has been influenced not only by the changing paradigm in monetary economics but also by the developments in the financial market and macroeconomic outcomes. In the event of adverse developments, the adequacy of extant economic policies is put to test as was during the recent global financial crisis. Crises are not desirable but they seem unavoidable. They do, however, provide us an opportunity for assessing various tenets of the extant policy framework. Against this backdrop, let me highlight our approach to financial stability.

Even before the crisis, institutional arrangement in the financial sector was already in place for inter-regulatory coordination for monitoring financial stability in the economy. A High Level Coordination Committee on Financial Markets (HLCCFM) was set up in 1992 with the Governor of the RBI as its Chairman, and the chiefs of the Securities and Exchange Board of India (SEBI), the Insurance Regulatory and Development Authority (IRDA) and the Pension Fund Regulatory and Development Authority (PFRDA), and the finance secretary to the Government of India as members. However, post-crisis, the collegial approach to financial stability has been further strengthened by constituting the Financial Stability and Development Council (FSDC).

FSDC, headed by the finance minister, was set up in December 2010 in the wake of the global financial crisis with a specific mandate, inter alia, for systemic financial stability. FSDC is expected to deal with issues relating to financial stability, developing the financial sector, inter-regulatory co-ordination and macro-prudential supervision of the economy including the functioning of large financial conglomerates. A sub-committee of FSDC, headed by the Governor of the RBI, replaced the HLCCFM and is the primary operating arm of the FSDC. This sub-committee has also set up a dedicated crisis management framework.

In addition, various committees of the RBI's central board monitor financial stability issues: the Board for Financial Supervision reviews the RBI's supervisory and regulatory initiatives and the Board for Payment and Settlement Systems oversees the overall functioning of the payment system.

Another development signifying the RBI's role in the context of financial stability is the setting up of a Financial Stability Unit in the bank in July 2009 with a mandate of conducting an effective macro-prudential surveillance of the financial system on an ongoing basis and enabling early detection of any incipient signs of instability. The RBI also brings out biannual financial stability reports. Incidentally, the IMF has recently concluded a financial sector assessment programme, which in fact comes close on the heels of a comprehensive self-assessment of the financial sector carried out by the RBI.

The RBI is one of those central banks which recognizes financial stability as one of the objectives of monetary policy and which has been vindicated by the crisis, with an increasing number of central banks giving greater attention to financial stability. While there is a broad consensus that financial stability should be an objective of central banks, it is not clear if it should be a direct objective of monetary policy. Multiple objectives call for multiple instruments. In this context, macro-prudential instruments of risk weights and provisioning are considered better suited than the interest rate, a key element of monetary policy. Can monetary policy lean against the wind of financial excesses? Some academics and central banks agree that in extreme stress situations, the interest rate could be used in conjunction with macro-prudential instruments to address the underlying vulnerability.

The taste of the pudding is in eating. How have the changes that have been made to the policy framework affected the economic outcome? This is an issue which I turn to with a focus on the more recent period.

Growth-inflation performance

In the 13-year monetary targeting during 1985–98, the real gross domestic product (GDP) increased at the rate of 5.5 per cent per annum, wholesale price (WPI) inflation increased by 8.1 per cent per annum and consumer price (CPI) inflation increased by 9.1 per cent per annum. In the following 11-year period of a multiple indicators approach during 1998–2010, GDP increased at a higher rate of 7 per cent per annum, WPI inflation moderated to 5.3 per cent per annum and CPI inflation declined to 6.3 per cent per annum. The period of the multiple indicators approach also encompassed a period of very high growth and even lower inflation. During the five-year period 2003–08, GDP growth averaged 8.7 per cent per annum, WPI inflation averaged 5.5 per cent per annum and CPI inflation was even lower at 5 per cent per annum.

These growth-inflation outcomes underscore the importance of price stability for securing higher growth. The credit for good performance cannot be attributed to monetary policy alone. The period 2003–08 witnessed considerable fiscal consolidation, which opened up the space for monetary policy to address the credit needs of the private sector. If fiscal and monetary policies work in tandem, the economic outcome can certainly be better.

Both growth and inflation performance has deteriorated in the post-crisis period since 2010–11. During the most recent four-year period, 2010–14, the average annual GDP growth declined to 6.5 per cent with the growth rate projected at 4.9 per cent in 2013–14. WPI inflation rate averaged 8.1 per cent per annum and CPI inflation rose to 9.8 per cent per annum. There are several explanations for why growth has declined and inflation has risen, which I do not intend to dwell on in detail. Explanations range from supply-side constraints to policy uncertainties to demand-side persistence of monetary and fiscal stimulus instituted immediately following the crisis. In this context, it is important to recognize that the recent inflation surge followed the global financial crisis. Managing inflation in an economy which is recovering from a downturn is much more complex because of associated uncertainties than managing inflation under normal conditions.

The Indian economy appeared to be stabilizing in 2013–14, with fiscal consolidation, clearance of many large investment projects, a good monsoon and moderation in inflation. However, volatility in the financial market returned following the announcement in May 2013 of the US Fed's intention of likely tapering of quantitative easing (QE). Portfolio outflows, particularly from the domestic currency debt segment, were substantial. This prompted the RBI to resort to somewhat unconventional monetary policy measures besides drawing down of foreign exchange reserves to meet the immediate shortfall. As portfolio capital outflows waned and BoP improved, stability returned to the foreign exchange market. This prompted the RBI to unwind a bulk of the exceptional measures and normalize monetary policy by restoring the policy interest rate corridor to its original configuration and the repo rate to its signalling role of policy. Currently, there are some signs of recovery in growth and moderation of inflationary pressures. Thus, in the post-crisis period though growth has moderated and inflation has risen, macro-stability has been maintained, which should provide the foundation for a durable recovery.

Monetary governance

Let me conclude with some thoughts on the governance aspects of macro-policies. Forming monetary policy is an ever-evolving process both in response to and as a consequence of changes in financial markets and the real economy. This is a phenomenon we have observed in India in our monetary policy formulation over the years. In the process, monetary policy in India has become increasingly transparent with greater involvement of all the stakeholders for better policy outcomes.

The government has been proactive in equipping the RBI with legislative changes to better address the evolving challenges. For example, in 1997, the government through an agreement stopped the practice of automatic monetization of fiscal deficit, which was a major source of money creation. This in a sense gave the much needed instrument independence to the RBI so that it could better deploy monetary policy instruments for growth inflation outcomes. Subsequent legislative changes have empowered the RBI to set CRR and SLR without a floor or ceiling. Currently, CRR is at 4 per cent, the lowest since the 1960s. SLR has been placed at 23 per cent of banks' NDTL with the RBI giving the flexibility of an additional two percentage points for the banks to access liquidity at the MSF rate at the LAF window.

With regard to the predominant objective of price stability, it can be argued that the RBI does not have the de jure independence of setting an inflation target. But this has not detracted it from articulating an inflation goal of 5 per cent per annum in the short-run and 3 per cent in the medium-term. Moreover, given the low inflation tolerance of our society, there is a de facto mandate for price stability, which is understood well by the government and the RBI. The apparent difference between the government and the RBI on monetary policy issues sometimes highlighted by the media is more in the nature of pace and sequencing than questioning the fundamental tenets. On broad macro-policy issues, the government is as committed to price stability as the RBI. Similarly, the government is also as concerned about fiscal consolidation as the RBI.

With regard to financial stability, financial markets and institutions have grown in complexity, the oversight and regulation of which could be beyond a single entity such as the central bank. Hence, financial stability will have to be a joint responsibility, though the central bank could have a dominant role by virtue of its being the natural lender of last resort. The RBI being the regulator and supervisor of banks, the payment system, the money market, the foreign exchange market and the government securities market automatically has a critical role in financial stability. The RBI has reinforced this process by internally re-organizing itself and periodically releasing a financial stability report in the public domain. The government has enhanced the framework and coordination mechanism by instituting FSDC.

The role of institutions is of paramount importance in a democracy. While everything cannot be anticipated and written as a law, the convention and practices developed by institutions become important. In this regard, the RBI has evolved as one of the most respected institutions in India with the active support of the government. The RBI also continues to reform itself through acquisition of skills and structure so that it can best deliver on its core mandate.

References

Schmitt-Grohe, Stephanie and Martin Uribe. (2011). 'The Optimal Rate of Inflation', in B. Friedman and M. Woodford (eds), *Handbook of Monetary Economics*. North-Holland.

Mohanty, Deepak, A.B. Chakraborty, Abhiman Das and Joice John. (2011).'Inflation Threshold in India: An empirical investigation', *RBI Working Paper Series, 18*.

Pattanaik, Sitikantha and G.V. Nadhanael. (2011).'Why Persistent High Inflation Impedes Growth? An Empirical Assessment of Threshold Level of Inflation in India', *RBI Working Paper Series, 17*.

Contributor Notes

Meghnad Desai is Emeritus Professor of Economics at LSE. He has written over 25 books including *Marx's Revenge*, *The Rediscovery of India* and *Who Wrote the Bhagavad Gita?: A Secular Inquiry into a Sacred Text*. He is a member of the House of Lords.

Dipankar Gupta is Distinguished Professor, Shiv Nadar University and Director of the Centre for Public Affairs and Critical Theory there. He taught in JNU for nearly 30 years, and in several universities in India and abroad. He has authored and/or edited 18 books, the latest being *Revolution from Above: India's Future and the Citizen Elite*.

Poonam Gupta is a Senior Economist at the World Bank, Washington DC. She has previously worked at the NIPFP (RBI Chair Professor), International Monetary Fund and Delhi School of Economics. Her research has been published in leading academic journals and has been featured in *The Economist*, *Financial Times*, and *Wall Street Journal*.

Ashima Goyal, Professor at IGIDR, Mumbai, is widely published in institutional and open economy macroeconomics, international finance and governance. She has received many fellowships, national and international awards, is active in the Indian public debate, and has served on several boards and policy committees.

Currently she is a member of the Technical Advisory Committee on the monetary policy of the RBI and edits a Routledge journal.

Ravi Kanbur is the T. H. Lee Professor of World Affairs at Cornell University. He is President of the Society for the Study of Economic Inequality, and a member of the OECD High Level Expert Group on the Measurement of Economic Performance. He has served on the senior staff of the World Bank including as Director of the World Development Report.

Sunil Mani is Planning Commission Chair Professor at the Centre for Development Studies, Trivandrum. His most recent book is an edited one with Richard Nelson, *TRIPS Compliance, National Patent Regimes and Innovation*.

T.T. Ram Mohan is Professor of Finance and Economics at IIM Ahmedabad. He is a graduate of IIT Bombay, IIM Calcutta and the Stern School, New York. He has authored five books and been a columnist for *The Economic Times* for 15 years. His association with various corporate boards over the years has given him a ring-side view of corporate governance.

Deepak Mohanty is Executive Director, Reserve Bank of India overseeing the area of monetary policy, economic research and statistics. Prior to his current position, he was Senior Adviser in the IMF and earlier worked in economic research and monetary policy departments of the RBI. He holds Master's degrees in Economics from Yale University and JNU.

Samuel Paul, founder of Public Affairs Centre at Bangalore, is a former Professor of Economics and Director of the Indian Institute of Management, Ahmedabad. He has also served as advisor to the World Bank in Washington and as special advisor to the UN Commission on Transnational Corporations. His latest book (editor) is *Fighting Corruption: The Way Forward* (2013).

M. Govinda Rao is a Member of the Fourteenth Finance Commission, Government of India. His past positions include Director, National Institute of Public Finance and Policy, New Delhi (2003-2012); Director, Institute for Social and Economic Change, Bangalore (1998-2002); and Fellow, Research School of Pacific and Asian Studies, Australian National University, Australia.

Index